HAMLYN ALL COLOUR
ORIENTAL COOKBOOK

TED SMART

Front jacket shows, clockwise from top right:
Kofta in Yogurt (113), *Semolina Barfi* (249), *Fish and Watercress
Soup* (1), *Grilled Spiced Fish* (69)

Back jacket shows, clockwise from top right:
Vinegared Cucumber (229), *Dhai Bhindi* (25), *Stir-Fried Lemony
Chicken* (165), *Parent-Child Bowl* (205)

This edition published in 1992
by Octopus Illustrated Publishing
part of Reed International Books
for The Book People
Guardian House, Borough Road
Godalming, Surrey GU7 2AE
© Copyright Reed International Books Limited 1989

Line drawings by Lorna Turpin

ISBN 1-85613-140-8
Produced by Mandarin Offset
Printed and bound in Hong Kong

Contents

Soups, Starters and Snacks   1–24

Vegetable and Pulse Dishes   25–68

Fish and Seafood Dishes   69–112

Meat Dishes   113–164

Poultry Dishes   165–204

Rice, Noodles and Breads   205–228

Salads and Side Dishes   229–248

Desserts   249–272

Useful Facts and Figures

Notes on metrication

In this book quantities are given in metric and Imperial measures. Exact conversion from Imperial to metric measures does not usually give very convenient working quantities and so the metric measures have been rounded off into units of 25 grams. The table below shows the recommended equivalents.

Ounces	Approx g to nearest whole figure	Recommended conversion to nearest unit of 25	Ounces	Approx g to nearest whole figure	Recommended conversion to nearest unit of 25
1	28	25	9	255	250
2	57	50	10	283	275
3	85	75	11	312	300
4	113	100	12	340	350
5	142	150	13	368	375
6	170	175	14	396	400
7	198	200	15	425	425
8	227	225	16 (1 lb)	454	450

Note: When converting quantities over 16 oz first add the appropriate figures in the centre column, then adjust to the nearest unit of 25. As a general guide, 1 kg (1000 g) equals 2.2 lb or about 2 lb 3 oz. This method of conversion gives good results in nearly all cases, although in certain pastry and cake recipes a more accurate conversion is necessary to produce a balanced recipe.

Liquid measures The millilitre has been used in this book and the following table gives a few examples.

Imperial	Approx ml to nearest whole figure	Recommended ml	Imperial	Approx ml to nearest whole figure	Recommended ml
$\frac{1}{4}$	142	150 ml	1 pint	567	600 ml
$\frac{1}{2}$	283	300 ml	1$\frac{1}{2}$ pints	851	900 ml
$\frac{3}{4}$	425	450 ml	1$\frac{3}{4}$ pints	992	1000 ml (1 litre)

Spoon measures All spoon measures given in this book are level unless otherwise stated.

Can sizes At present, cans are marked with the exact (usually to the nearest whole number) metric equivalent of the Imperial weight of the contents, so we have followed this practice when giving can sizes.

Oven temperatures
The table below gives recommended equivalents.

	°C	°F	Gas Mark		°C	°F	Gas Mark
Very cool	110	225	$\frac{1}{4}$	Moderately hot	190	375	5
	120	250	$\frac{1}{2}$		200	400	6
Cool	140	275	1	Hot	220	425	7
	150	300	2		230	450	8
Moderate	160	325	3	Very Hot	240	475	9
	180	350	4				

Notes for American and Australian users

In America the 8-fl oz measuring cup is used. In Australia metric measures are now used in conjunction with the standard 250-ml measuring cup. The Imperial pint, used in Britain and Australia, is 20 fl oz, while the American pint is 16 fl oz. It is important to remember that the Australian tablespoon differs from both the British and American tablespoons; the table below gives a comparison. The British standard tablespoon, which has been used throughout this book, holds 17.7 ml, the American 14.2 ml, and the Australian 20 ml. A teaspoon holds approximately 5 ml in all three countries.

British	American	Australian
1 teaspoon	1 teaspoon	1 teaspoon
1 tablespoon	1 tablespoon	1 tablespoon
2 tablespoons	3 tablespoons	2 tablespoons
3$\frac{1}{2}$ tablespoons	4 tablespoons	3 tablespoons
4 tablespoons	5 tablespoons	3$\frac{1}{2}$ tablespoons

An Imperial/American guide to solid and liquid measures

Imperial	American	Imperial	American
Solid measures		**Liquid measures**	
1 lb butter or		$\frac{1}{4}$ pint liquid	$\frac{2}{3}$ cup liquid
margarine	2 cups	$\frac{1}{2}$ pint	1$\frac{1}{4}$ cups
1 lb flour	4 cups	$\frac{3}{4}$ pint	2 cups
1 lb granulated or		1 pint	2$\frac{1}{2}$ cups
caster sugar	2 cups	1$\frac{1}{2}$ pints	3$\frac{3}{4}$ cups
1 lb icing sugar	3 cups	2 pints	5 cups
8 oz rice	1 cup		(2$\frac{1}{2}$ pints)

Note: When making any of the recipes in this book, only follow one set of measures as they are not interchangeable.

Introduction

The subject of oriental cookery is immensely rich and varied. In the Hamlyn All Colour Oriental Cookbook there is an invaluable collection of recipes encompassing the cuisines of India, China, Japan, Korea and South-east Asia making this a unique collection for aspiring oriental cooks. The eight chapters will take you on a culinary journey not only through the countries mentioned but will also give you insight into the customs, traditions and history of many of the dishes and, perhaps more importantly, when to serve them and what with.

A colour photograph illustrates each recipe so that you can see the result you are aiming for and also pick up ideas for authentic or dazzling garnishes. In addition short cuts, dietary information, cook ahead pointers or food ingredient explanations are provided in the Cook's Tips which appear below each recipe. Every recipe will also give you a calorie counted assessment of a portion size to assist in health-conscious and weight-conscious meal planning.

Preparation and cooking times given at the beginning of each recipe will also tell you at a glance whether you have time to cook a recipe today or whether you should plan it ahead for tomorrow.

Oriental cookery newcomers will also find valuable information in the Cook's Tips regarding unfamiliar or obscure ingredients. Don't be put off by any obscure-sounding ingredients – most large supermarkets will stock many of them and the smaller Oriental and Asian grocers and specialist supermarkets are bound to head you in the right direction.

The chapter sequence it is hoped will be of immense help when planning a complete menu – beginning with starters, soups and snacks, through main course and side dish vegetable and pulse dishes, to main course anchors in fish and seafood, meat or poultry, taking in a whole host of rice, noodle, bread, dumpling, salads and accompaniments to finally crowning the meal with a delicious selection of desserts and sweetmeats. Along the way you may decide to stick to just one cuisine, like Chinese or Indian, or alternatively island-hop around South-east Asia to experience the many culinary delights of cultures so near yet so enticingly diverse.

Good eating!

Soups, Starters and Snacks

From the spicy exuberance of the Indian pakora to the mild, subtle taste of a Chinese wonton, the importance of the starter has long been recognized in the Orient. Here are some delicious meat, fish and vegetable starters, soups and snacks to entice and delight the palate.

1 | Fish and Watercress Soup

(Illustrated on front jacket)

Preparation time
15 minutes

Cooking time
about 5–10 minutes

Serves 4

Calories
80 per portion

You will need
225 g/8 oz white fish fillets (plaice, sole or cod, for example)
1 tablespoon cornflour
1 egg white, lightly beaten
600 ml/1 pint clear stock
1 teaspoon finely chopped fresh root ginger
1 bunch watercress, washed and trimmed
salt and pepper
1 teaspoon finely shredded spring onion
1 teaspoon sesame oil

Cut the fish into large slices. Dust with the cornflour, then coat with the egg white.

Pour the stock into a saucepan, add the ginger and bring to a rolling boil. Add the fish, a slice at a time. As soon as the slices float to the surface, add the watercress and seasoning to taste. Reduce the heat and simmer for 1 minute.

Pour the soup into warmed serving bowls and sprinkle the tops with the shredded spring onion and sesame oil. Serve hot.

2 | Mulligatawny Soup

Preparation time
30 minutes

Cooking time
about 3 hours

Serves 6

Calories
410 per portion

You will need
450 g/1 lb shin of beef, cubed
1 kg/2 lb beef bones
about 2.25 litres /4 pints water
1 tablespoon coriander seeds
½ teaspoon black peppercorns
2 teaspoons cumin seeds
1 teaspoon turmeric
6 green cardamom pods
2–3 cloves
4 cloves garlic, crushed
salt
2 potatoes, peeled and diced
1 tablespoon oil
1 large onion, finely sliced
1 teaspoon garam masala
600 ml/1 pint coconut milk (see Cook's Tip)
juice of 1 lemon

Place the beef and bones and water in a pan. Add the coriander seeds, peppercorns, cumin, turmeric, cardamoms, cloves and garlic with salt to taste. Bring to the boil, skim, then cover and simmer for 2 hours. Cool slightly. Discard the bones and shred the meat finely.

Strain the soup and remove the spices. Return 1.75 litres/3 pints of the soup to the pan, add the potatoes and cook for 20 minutes. Stir in the reserved meat and set aside.

Heat the oil and fry the onion until golden. Add the garam masala, remove from the heat and stir in the coconut milk. Stir into the soup, add the lemon juice and re-heat without boiling to serve.

Cook's Tip

It isn't necessary to skin the fish fillets; the skin helps to keep the fish intact during cooking.

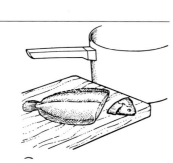

Cook's Tip

Make the coconut milk by placing 225 g/8 oz desiccated coconut and 750 ml/1¼ pints boiling water in a food processor or liquidizer. Blend for 20 seconds then pour into a bowl and cool to blood heat. Strain the milk into a clean bowl. Squeeze the coconut firmly over the sieve to obtain the coconut milk.

3 | Fish Soup with Coconut

Preparation time
25 minutes

Cooking time
about 15–20 minutes

Serves 4

Calories
420 per portion

You will need
550 g/1¼ lb monkfish or halibut
   fillet, skinned and cubed
salt
25 g/1 oz desiccated coconut
6 shallots
6 almonds, blanched
2–3 cloves garlic
2.5 cm/1 inch piece root ginger,
   peeled and sliced
2 stems lemon grass, trimmed
   and root discarded
2–3 teaspoons turmeric
3 tablespoons oil
1 recipe coconut cream and milk
   (see Cook's Tip)
1–2 fresh chillies, seeded and
   finely sliced
fresh coriander to garnish

Sprinkle the fish with salt. Place the coconut in a wok and heat until golden and crisp. Remove and pound until oily. Purée the shallots, almonds, garlic, ginger and 6 cm/2½ inches from the root end of the lemon grass (reserve the remainder) in a blender. Add the turmeric.

Heat the oil and fry the puréed mixture for a few minutes. Add the coconut milk and bring to the boil, stirring constantly. Add the fish, chillies, remaining lemon grass and cook for 3–4 minutes. Stir in the pounded coconut and cook for 2–3 minutes. Remove the stems of lemon grass, stir in the coconut cream, transfer to a serving tureen and garnish with fresh coriander.

Cook's Tip

To make the coconut cream and milk for the recipe above, put 300 g/11 oz desiccated coconut and 750 ml/1¼ pints boiling water in a blender and work for 20 seconds. Pour into a bowl and cool to blood heat. Strain the milk into a bowl; this is the coconut milk. The squeezed out flesh is the pounded coconut for adding later. When the cream rises to the top of the coconut milk skim off about 50 ml/2 fl oz and add to the soup just before serving.

4 | Corn and Fish Soup

Preparation time
10 minutes plus 10
minutes marinating
time

Cooking time
about 10 minutes

Serves 4

Calories
180 per portion

You will need
450 g/1 lb filleted white fish (cod
   or sea bass for example)
1 teaspoon ginger juice (see
   Cook's Tip)
1 teaspoon sherry
salt
900 ml/1½ pints water
1 (225-g/8-oz) can sweetcorn,
   drained
1 teaspoon oil
1½ teaspoons cornflour mixed
   with 1 tablespoon water
1 spring onion, chopped

Place the fish in a shallow heatproof dish with the ginger juice, sherry and a generous pinch of salt. Leave to marinate for 10 minutes. Place in a steamer and steam for 5–6 minutes. Remove from the heat and mash the fish with a fork. Set aside.

Pour the water into a large saucepan and bring to the boil. Add the sweetcorn, oil and 1 teaspoon salt. Simmer for 2 minutes. Add the cornflour mixture and cook, stirring, until the soup thickens. Add the fish and cook for 1 minute. Pour into soup bowls and serve hot sprinkled with the spring onion.

Cook's Tip

Root ginger is used extensively in oriental cooking. To extract ginger juice from the root, place small peeled slices of root ginger in a garlic crusher and squeeze firmly.

5 | *Prawn and Squid Hot Soup*

Preparation time
20 minutes

Cooking time
about 10 minutes

Serves 4

Calories
100 per portion

You will need
225 g/8 oz squid
1.8 litres/3 pints stock
3 lime leaves
1 stem lemon grass, crushed
225 g/8 oz prawns, peeled
nam pla (fish sauce) to taste (see Cook's Tip)
2–4 fresh chillies, sliced into rounds
2 cloves garlic, crushed
juice of 1 lime or lemon
chopped fresh coriander leaves, to garnish

Clean the squid, cut off and chop the tentacles; cut the body into rings.

Put the stock, lime leaves and lemon grass in a pan, bring to the boil, lower the heat and simmer for 5 minutes. Add the prawns, squid and nam pla. Cook until the prawns turn pink, then add the chillies.

Pour the soup into 4 warmed individual bowls. Mix together the garlic and lime or lemon juice to taste, then stir into the soup. Sprinkle with the coriander and serve hot.

6 | *Pork, Ham and Bamboo Shoot Soup*

Preparation time
about 20 minutes

Cooking time
about 10–15 minutes

Serves 4

Calories
70 per portion

You will need
50 g/2 oz pork fillet
2 teaspoons soy sauce
50 g/2 oz cooked ham
50 g/2 oz bamboo shoots
600 ml/1 pint clear broth (see Cook's Tip recipe 10)
1 teaspoon salt
1 teaspoon sherry

Thinly slice the pork and mix it with the soy sauce. Shred the ham and bamboo shoots.

Bring the stock to the boil, put in the pork, ham and bamboo shoots. When the soup starts to boil again, add the salt and sherry and serve hot.

Cook's Tip

Nam pla or Indonesian fish sauce is prepared from fresh anchovies and salt which are layered in wooden barrels and left to ferment. The liquid that is drained off is the fish sauce and is highly prized in Indonesian cuisine. It is **available from oriental stores and specialist shops.**

Cook's Tip

If you prefer a thicker soup simply mix 2 teaspoons cornflour to a smooth paste with 1 tablespoon water and stir into the soup at the end. Cook for 1–2 minutes to thicken.

7 | *Soup with Fresh Greens*

Preparation time
15 minutes

Cooking time
10–15 minutes

Serves 4

Calories
50 per portion

You will need
1.2 litres/2 pints water
1 onion, sliced
3 cloves garlic, sliced
3 tablespoons pounded dried
  shrimps
½ teaspoon shrimp paste
  (optional)
2 teaspoons soy sauce
1 teaspoon salt
225 g/8 oz fresh green leaves,
  washed (see Cook's Tip)

Put the water, onion and garlic in a large pan and bring to the boil. Lower the heat, then add the shrimps, shrimp paste, if used, soy sauce and salt. Stir well, then add the green leaves.

  Boil for 5 minutes, taste and adjust the seasoning, then pour into a warmed soup tureen. Serve hot.

8 | *Chicken and Sweetcorn Soup*

Preparation time
10 minutes

Cooking time
20–25 minutes

Serves 4

Calories
120 per portion

You will need
900 ml/1½ pints clear broth (see
  Cook's Tip recipe 10) with a
  little of the cooked chicken
  reserved
350 g/12 oz sweetcorn kernels
salt and pepper
2 teaspoons cornflour (optional)
1 tablespoon water (optional)
chopped spring onions to garnish
  (optional)

Pour the skimmed stock into a large pan and add 225 g/8oz of the sweetcorn. Bring to the boil, add salt and pepper to taste, cover and simmer for 15 minutes. Blend the soup in a liquidizer or food processor until smooth, then return to the pan.

  Reheat the soup and decide whether it is thick enough for your liking. If not, blend the cornflour with the water and stir it into the soup, then bring to the boil. Add the remaining sweetcorn and the reserved chopped chicken from preparing the stock. Simmer for 5 minutes, then taste and adjust the seasoning before serving, garnished with spring onions if liked.

Cook's Tip

This is an everyday soup which is quick and very easy to make. The dried shrimps can be pounded at home or bought ready-powdered, and the soup can be varied by adding different fresh green vegetable leaves: watercress, *sorrel, spinach, cabbage, pea leaves or mustard leaves.*

Cook's Tip

Crisp prawn crackers make a very tasty accompaniment to this soup.

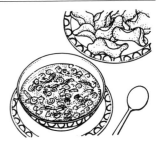

9 | Spiced Chicken Soup

Preparation time
20 minutes

Cooking time
about 1¼ hours

Serves 4–6

Calories
480–320 per portion

You will need
1.5 litres/2½ pints water
1.2 kg/2½ lb chicken, quartered
4 green King prawns, halved
salt and pepper
2 macadamias, chopped
4 shallots, chopped
2 garlic cloves, chopped
2 teaspoons grated root ginger
pinch of turmeric
pinch of chilli powder
vegetable oil for shallow frying
1 tablespoon light soy sauce
about 75 g/3 oz beansprouts
1 potato, peeled and cut into very
    thin rounds

Place the water in a pan and boil. Add the chicken, prawns and salt and pepper to taste. Cover and simmer for 40 minutes. Strain and reserve 1.2 litres/2 pints of the liquid. Shred the meat from the chicken and shell and chop the prawns.

Purée the macadamias, shallots, garlic and ginger in a liquidizer, add the turmeric and chilli and mix well.

Heat 2 tablespoons oil in a wok or frying pan, add the spice paste and fry for a few seconds. Stir in 300 ml/½ pint of the reserved liquid, the soy sauce, chicken and prawns. Simmer for 10 minutes. Add the remaining cooking liquid and simmer for a further 10 minutes. Add the beansprouts and cook for 3 minutes. Meanwhile, fry the potato slices in hot oil until crisp. Serve hot.

Cook's Tip

Macadamias are pale yellow nuts, roughly the same size as chestnuts. They are usually ready shelled and the kernels break into fragments. If 2 kemiri are specified in a recipe, this means the equivalent of 2 whole nuts.

10 | Shrimp Wonton Soup

Preparation time
30 minutes

Cooking time
10–15 minutes

Serves 4–6

Calories
140–95 per portion

You will need
40 sheets wonton wrappings
1.2 litres/2 pints clear broth (see
    Cook's Tip)
1 spring onion, chopped

For the filling
1 egg
1 teaspoon dry sherry
1 teaspoon salt
pinch of pepper
2 teaspoons oil
½ teaspoon sugar
1 tablespoon cornflour
225 g/8 oz prawns, shelled and
    chopped
100 g/4 oz fresh or canned
    waterchestnuts, drained and
    chopped

To make the filling, mix the egg, sherry, salt, pepper, oil, sugar and cornflour in a bowl. Mix in the prawns and waterchestnuts. Place ½ teaspoon filling in the centre of each wonton wrapping, moisten the edges with water, fold corner to corner into a triangle and seal, then seal the bottom corners together like a nun's hat.

Cook the wonton, a few at a time, in boiling water until they float on the surface, then transfer to the hot broth. Serve hot, sprinkled with the chopped spring onion.

Cook's Tip

To make clear broth, place 1 meaty chicken carcass, 675 g/1½ lb pork spareribs, 450 g/1 lb ham, bacon or beef bones, 2 litres/3½ pints water, 2 teaspoons salt and 2 teaspoons dried shrimps (optional) in a large pan. Bring to the boil, cover and simmer gently for 1¾ hours, skimming frequently. Leave to cool. When cold, skim any fat from the surface. Reheat and use as required.

11 | *Amotik*

Preparation time
*15 minutes, plus 30
minutes soaking time*

Cooking time
20–25 minutes

Serves 4

Calories
300 per portion

You will need
*50 g/2 oz tamarind (see Cook's
    Tip)
6 tablespoons hot water
4 tablespoons oil
675 g/1½ lb monkfish or other
    firm white fish, cubed
flour for dusting
1 onion, chopped
4 green chillies, finely chopped
2 garlic cloves, crushed
1 teaspoon ground cumin
½–1 teaspoon chilli powder
salt
1 tablespoon vinegar*

Soak the tamarind in the water for 30 minutes, then strain, squeezing out as much water as possible. Discard the tamarind and reserve the water.

Heat the oil in a large pan. Lightly dust the fish with flour, add to the pan and fry quickly on both sides. Remove from the pan with a slotted spoon and set aside.

Add the onion to the pan and fry until soft and golden. Add the tamarind water, chillies, garlic, cumin, chilli powder and salt to taste and cook for 10 minutes. Add the fish and any juices and the vinegar. Simmer, uncovered, for about 5 minutes; be careful not to overcook.

12 | *Crispy Spring Rolls*

Preparation time
20–25 minutes

Cooking time
about 15–20 minutes

Serves 4–6

Calories
540–400 per portion

You will need
*225 g/8 oz plain flour
pinch of salt
1 egg
oil for deep frying*

*For the filling
1 tablespoon oil
225 g/8 oz lean pork, shredded
1 garlic clove, crushed
2 celery sticks, sliced
100 g/4 oz mushrooms, sliced
2 spring onions, chopped
100 g/4 oz beansprouts
100 g/4 oz peeled prawns
2 tablespoons soy sauce*

Sift the flour and salt into a bowl. Add the egg and about 300 ml/½ pint water to make a smooth batter. Lightly oil a 20-cm/8-inch frying pan and place over a moderate heat. Pour in enough batter to cover the base of the pan. Cook until the underside is pale golden, then turn and cook on the other side. Remove from the pan and repeat with the remaining batter.

To make the filling, heat the oil in a pan, add the pork and brown quickly. Add the garlic and vegetables; stir-fry for 2 minutes. Mix in the prawns and soy sauce. Leave until cool.

Place 2–3 tablespoons of the filling in the centre of each pancake. Fold in the sides and form to a tight roll, sticking down the edge with a little flour and water paste. Heat the oil and deep fry until golden.

Cook's Tip

**Tamarind are the pods from
the tamarind tree, used as a
souring agent. They are sold
as pods or pulp. Either must
be soaked in hot water, then
squeezed and strained before
use. Vinegar or lemon juice
may be used instead.**

Cook's Tip

**Ideally use fresh beansprouts,
the tiny, crunchy shoots of
mung beans, for this recipe.
They should be used on the
day of purchase. They are also
sold in cans but must be well
drained before use.**

13 | Fish Fritters

Preparation time
15–20 minutes, plus
standing time

Cooking time
10–15 minutes

Serves 4

Calories
250 per portion

You will need
6 tablespoons oil
2 onions, chopped
1 tablespoon ground coriander
3 green chillies, seeded and
    chopped
1 teaspoon salt
1 teaspoon pepper
675 g/1½ lb cod fillets, skinned
    and cut into small pieces
2 tablespoons finely chopped
    fresh coriander leaves

For the batter
100 g/4 oz gram flour (see Cook's
    Tip)
½ teaspoon chilli powder
½ teaspoon salt
1 egg, beaten
7 tablespoons water

Heat 3 tablespoons of the oil in a pan. Add the onions and
fry until just soft. Stir in the coriander, chillies, salt and
pepper, then add the fish. Fry for 2 minutes, then cover
and cook on a very low heat for 2 minutes. Break up the
mixture with a fork and add the chopped coriander. Set
aside.
  To make the batter, sift the flour, chilli powder and salt
into a bowl. Add the egg and water and beat to make a
smooth batter. Leave to stand for 30 minutes.
  Stir the fish mixture into the batter. Heat the remaining
oil in a frying pan and drop in small spoonfuls; fry on both
sides until golden. Drain the fritters thoroughly, then
serve while still warm.

Cook's Tip

**Gram flour, also called bessan,
is made from ground chick
peas or split peas. In Indian
cuisine it is used instead of
ordinary flour, especially for
making batters.**

14 | Ekuri

Preparation time
10 minutes

Cooking time
5–10 minutes

Serves 4

Calories
300 per portion

You will need
50 g/2 oz butter
1 onion, finely chopped
2 green chillies, finely chopped
8 eggs, lightly beaten with 2
    tablespoons water
1 tablespoon finely chopped fresh
    coriander leaves

Heat the butter in a pan, add the onion and fry until deep
golden. Add the chillies and fry for 30 seconds, then add
the eggs, coriander and salt to taste. Cook, stirring constantly, until the eggs are lightly scrambled and set.
Serve hot.

Cook's Tip

**Hot, fresh green chillies
should be used for this recipe,
but use with care. For a less
pungent result slit the chillies,
discard the seeds and rinse
under a tap. Do not touch
your face or eyes while
handling chillies.**

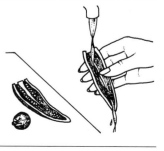

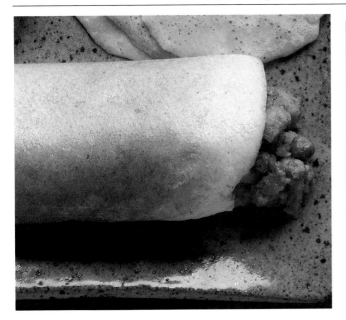

15 | *Dosas*

Preparation time
10 minutes, plus
overnight soaking time

Cooking time
about 20 minutes

Makes 12–15

Calories
120 per dosa

You will need
225 g/8 oz urhad dhal (dried
  pulses or lentils)
50 g/2 oz long-grain rice
600 ml/1 pint water
½ teaspoon bicarbonate of soda
1 teaspoon chilli powder
½ teaspoon salt
vegetable oil for shallow frying

Wash the dhal and rice thoroughly, then put in a bowl with the water and leave to soak overnight.

Place the dhal, rice and water mixture in a blender or food processor and work until smooth. Add the soda, chilli powder and salt and stir well.

Pour in enough batter to cover the bottom of a cold, heavy-based pan. Put on the heat until the batter starts to set. Pour about 1 tablespoon oil around the edge of the dosa, then shake the pan to spread the oil. Fry the pancake for about 1 minute, until golden underneath. Remove from the pan and roll up each dosa, enclosing a filling if liked. Repeat with the remaining batter. Serve hot.

16 | *Prawn and Beansprout Fritters*

Preparation time
20 minutes

Cooking time
about 2 minutes

Serves 6–8

Calories
180–140 per portion

You will need
100 g/4 oz peeled prawns,
  minced
225 g/8 oz beansprouts
4 shallots, thinly sliced
½ small onion, finely sliced
2 garlic cloves, crushed
2 tablespoons chopped fresh
  coriander leaves (optional)
2 teaspoons grated root ginger
2 tablespoons grated coconut
  flesh (optional)
50 g/2 oz rice flour or self-raising
  flour
1 teaspoon baking powder
1 teaspoon ground coriander
½ teaspoon chilli powder
3 tablespoons water
1 egg, beaten
salt and pepper
vegetable oil for deep frying
lemon slices to garnish

Put all the ingredients except the oil in a bowl and mix well. Form the mixture into small balls about the size of walnuts, or flatten them into burger shapes.

Heat the oil and fry the fritters for 1½–2 minutes until golden. Remove with a slotted spoon and drain on absorbent kitchen paper. Transfer to a serving dish and garnish with lemon slices. Serve hot or cold.

Cook's Tip

This is a great breakfast pancake from the south of India, eaten also as a snack throughout the day. Like pancakes, they can be eaten plain or with a savoury filling.

Cook's Tip

These Malaysian fritters are usually made without prawns, but their addition certainly makes the fritters tastier. Serve as a snack with drinks, or as a side dish with a rice meal.

17 | *Vietnamese Chicken Spring Rolls*

Preparation time
30 minutes

Cooking time
about 10 minutes

Makes 20

Calories
120 per roll

You will need
50 g/2 oz cellophane noodles,
  soaked in water for 10 minutes,
  then cut into 2.5-cm/1-inch
  pieces
450 g/1 lb chicken breast meat,
  cut into thin strips
2 tablespoons dried wood ears
  (see Cook's Tip), finely chopped
3 garlic cloves, finely chopped
3 shallots, finely chopped
225 g/8 oz crabmeat
½ teaspoon black pepper

For the wrappers
4 eggs, beaten
20 dried rice papers
450 ml/¾ pint vegetable oil
shredded green shallot to garnish

To make the filling, put all the ingredients in a bowl and mix well. Divide and shape into 20 small cylinder shapes.

Brush beaten egg over the entire surface of each piece of rice paper. Leave for a few minutes until soft. Place the filling along the curved edge of the paper, roll once, then fold over the sides to enclose and continue rolling.

Heat the oil and fry the spring rolls, one-third at a time, until golden. Drain thoroughly on absorbent kitchen paper. Serve hot or at room temperature, garnished with the shredded green shallot.

18 | *Samosas*

Preparation time
30 minutes

Cooking time
about 20 minutes

Makes about 24

Calories
200 per samosa

You will need
225 g/8 oz plain flour
3 tablespoons ghee
½ teaspoon salt
about 250 ml/8 fl oz milk, soured
  with a little lemon juice
vegetable oil for deep frying

For the filling
1 recipe Vegetable Kheema (see
  recipe 114)

Sift the flour into a bowl, rub in the ghee, then add the salt. Gradually stir in the milk to form a stiff dough. Chill until required.

Break the dough into pieces, about 2.5 cm/1 inch in diameter. Roll into very thin circles, then cut each circle in half. Spoon a little of the filling into the centre of each semi-circle, then fold in half to make a triangular cone shape, enclosing the filling. Moisten the edges of the dough with soured milk and seal well.

Heat the oil and deep fry the samosas, a few at a time, for about 1 minute until the pastry is golden. Drain well and serve warm.

Cook's Tip

Wood ear is a dried fern fungus, known as cloud ear in China, and is available at Chinese supermarkets. Before using, soak the wood ears for about 20 minutes until they become glutinous and crinkly.

Cook's Tip

These small pastries are good to serve with pre-dinner drinks. In India they are usually eaten as a snack – often served with tea. They keep quite well in an airtight container in the refrigerator and can be reheated under a preheated hot grill before serving.

19 | *Wonton*

Preparation time
25 minutes

Cooking time
5 minutes

Serves 4–6

Calories
800–560 per portion

You will need
450 g/1 lb wonton paste
450 g/1 lb minced streaky pork
2 tablespoons soy sauce
1 teaspoon brown sugar
1 teaspoon salt
350 g/12 oz frozen leaf spinach,
    thawed
oil for deep frying

Cut out 5-cm/2-inch rounds from the wonton paste. Put the pork, soy sauce, sugar and salt in a bowl and mix well. Squeeze the spinach in a clean cloth to extract as much liquid as possible, then add to the pork mixture and mix thoroughly.

Place a little of the pork and spinach mixture in the centre of each wonton paste round. Dampen the edges, fold over the filling and press together to seal.

Heat the oil to 180 C/350 F and deep fry the wonton for about 5 minutes until golden. Drain on absorbent kitchen paper. Serve hot, with soy sauce.

Cook's Tip

Wonton paste, or wonton skin as it is sometimes called, is available from most Chinese stores.

20 | *Pakoras*

Preparation time
20 minutes, plus 2
hours standing time

Cooking time
about 10 minutes

Serves 4

Calories
180 per portion

You will need
150 g/5 oz gram flour or bessan
    (see Cook's Tip recipe 13)
½ teaspoon chilli powder
½ teaspoon salt
150 ml/¼ pint natural yogurt
1 teaspoon lemon juice
vegetable oil for deep frying

For the filling
about 350 g/12 oz chopped mixed
    vegetables (cauliflower florets,
    cubed aubergine, sliced green
    peppers and sliced courgettes
    for example)

Sift the flour into a bowl, rubbing any lumps through the sieve with the back of a spoon. Add the chilli powder and salt and mix well. Gradually stir in the yogurt and lemon juice. Cover and leave in a cool place for 2 hours until the batter is thick – it should be much thicker than pancake batter.

Dip the vegetable pieces in the batter to coat, then deep fry in hot oil until golden. Drain on absorbent kitchen paper. Serve while warm and fresh.

Cook's Tip

This batter may be cooked plain without the vegetables if liked. Pakoras will keep in an airtight container for a few days. Reheat under the grill before serving.

21 | Prawns and Eggs in Coconut Sauce

Preparation time
15 minutes

Cooking time
20 minutes

Serves 4

Calories
350 per portion

You will need
550 g/1¼ lb peeled large prawns
5 macadamias, chopped (see
  Cook's Tip recipe 9)
3 red chillies, seeded and
  chopped
1 small onion, chopped
2 garlic cloves, chopped
½ teaspoon dried shrimp paste
2 teaspoons ground coriander
1 teaspoon grated root ginger
2 tablespoons oil
3 ripe tomatoes, chopped
salt
1 bay leaf
150 ml/¼ pint water
150 ml/¼ pint thick coconut milk
4 hard-boiled eggs, halved
75 g/3 oz mangetout, trimmed

Halve and de-vein the prawns. Put the macadamias, chillies, onion, garlic, shrimp paste and ginger in a liquidizer or food processor and purée.

Heat the oil in a wok or frying pan and fry the paste for 1 minute, stirring constantly. Add the prawns, tomatoes and salt to taste. Stir, then cover and simmer for 2 minutes. Stir in the bay leaf and water. Increase the heat and boil, uncovered, for 5 minutes.

Lower the heat, add the coconut milk and eggs and simmer for 8 minutes. Add the mangetout and simmer for 3 minutes. Transfer to a warmed serving dish and garnish as shown.

Cook's Tip

King prawns have a fine flavour but they are expensive. Instead you can use small peeled-cooked prawns, in which case you will not have to de-vein them.

22 | Spiced Fried Prawns

Preparation time
15 minutes, plus 30
minutes marinating
time

Cooking time
about 10 minutes

Serves 4

Calories
300 per portion

You will need
450 g/1 lb cooked prawns
2 tablespoons tamarind water
  (see Cook's Tip recipe 11)
pinch of turmeric
1 teaspoon grated root ginger
2 shallots or ½ onion, sliced
2 garlic cloves, crushed
1 tablespoon light soy sauce
150 ml/¼ pint oil

For the batter
75 g/3 oz rice flour or plain flour
4 tablespoons water
salt and pepper
1 small egg, beaten

Discard the heads and shells from the prawns, but leave on the tails. De-vein them. Place in a bowl with the tamarind water, turmeric, ginger, shallots, garlic and soy sauce. Stir well and leave to marinate for 30 minutes.

Meanwhile, make the batter. Place the flour in a bowl and gradually add the water. Add salt and pepper to taste, then gradually beat in the egg.

Drain the marinade from the prawns and shallots. Dip the prawns and shallots in the batter. Heat the oil in a frying pan or wok and add the prawns and shallots, one at a time, until the bottom is covered. Fry until golden brown and crisp, then turn over and fry the underside. Serve hot or cold.

Cook's Tip

This dish should really be made with freshly cooked prawns, but is still delicious with pre-cooked prawns from the fishmonger. Serve as a snack or as a side dish with rice.

23 | Chicken Tikka

Preparation time
15 minutes, plus
overnight marinating
time

Cooking time
5–6 minutes

Serves 4

Calories
200 per portion

You will need
675 g/1½ lb chicken breasts

For the marinade
150 ml/¼ pint natural yogurt
1 tablespoon grated root ginger
2 garlic cloves, crushed
1 teaspoon chilli powder
1 tablespoon ground coriander
½ teaspoon salt
juice of 1 lemon
2 tablespoons oil

For the garnish
1 onion, sliced
2 tomatoes, quartered
4 lemon twists (see Cook's Tip)

Skin, bone and cube the chicken breasts. Mix all the marinade ingredients together in a bowl. Add the chicken cubes, stir well and leave in the refrigerator overnight.

Thread the chicken on to 4 skewers and cook under a preheated hot grill for 5–6 minutes, turning frequently.

Remove the chicken from the skewers and arrange on individual serving plates. Garnish with onion, tomato and lemon to serve.

24 | Meat Puffs

Preparation time
15 minutes, plus 1 hour
standing time

Cooking time
about 10 minutes

Serves 4

Calories
330 per portion

You will need
3 tablespoons self-raising flour
3 eggs, beaten
5–6 tablespoons water
225 g/8 oz minced beef
1 bunch spring onions, trimmed
  and finely sliced
1 green chilli, finely chopped
1 teaspoon turmeric
salt
vegetable oil for frying

Sift the flour into a bowl, add the eggs and beat well to combine. Gradually add enough water to make a thick, creamy batter, beating well.

Stir in the minced beef, onions, chilli, turmeric and salt to taste; the mixture should be like stiff porridge. Leave in a warm place for 1 hour.

Heat about 1 cm/½ inch depth of oil in a frying pan. When really hot drop in spoonfuls of the meat mixture and fry on each side for 2 minutes. Drain well and keep warm while cooking the remainder, adding more oil as required. Serve hot.

Cook's Tip

**To make lemon twists, thinly
slice a lemon and cut a slit in
to the centre of each slice.
Twist the slices from the cuts.**

Cook's Tip

**Turmeric is a rhizome
commonly used in its
powdered form for its earthy
taste and yellow colour. It
stains clothing and work
surfaces, so be careful not to
spill it.**

Vegetable and Pulse Dishes

Here you will find a bumper crop of stir-fried dishes, a host of carefully cooked and gently simmered curries, a feast of steamed or braised lentils and pulses and a medley of lightly cooked vegetables tossed in an array of sauces and seasonings.

25 | Dhai Bhindi

(Illustrated on back jacket)

Preparation time
15 minutes

Cooking time
15–20 minutes

Serves 4

Calories
70 per portion

You will need
225 g/8 oz okra
2 tablespoons oil
2.5 cm/1 inch piece root ginger, peeled and chopped
1 teaspoon turmeric
salt
2–3 tablespoons water
300 ml/½ pint natural yogurt
½ teaspoon chilli powder
2 tablespoons grated fresh coconut
1 tablespoon finely chopped fresh coriander leaves

Cut the tops off the okra and halve lengthways. Heat the oil in a pan, add the okra and fry for 5 minutes. Add the ginger, turmeric and salt to taste, stir well. Add the water, cover and cook for 10 minutes until the okra is tender.

Mix the remaining ingredients together. Add to the pan, stir well and serve.

26 | Dhal Sag

Preparation time
10 minutes

Cooking time
1 hour 10 minutes

Serves 4

Calories
370 per portion

You will need
225 g/8 oz moong dhal lentils, washed and drained
600 ml/1 pint water
3 onions, 1 sliced and 2 finely chopped
1 teaspoon chilli powder
½ teaspoon turmeric
salt
3 tablespoons oil
1 garlic clove, finely chopped
2 green chillies, finely chopped
2 teaspoons finely grated root ginger
1 teaspoon fennel seed
1 kg/2 lb spinach, washed and chopped

Put the dhal, water, sliced onion, chilli powder, turmeric and 1 teaspoon salt in a pan and bring to the boil, then partially cover the pan and simmer for 1 hour.

In another pan, heat the oil, add the chopped onions and garlic and fry until soft and golden. Stir in the chillies, ginger and fennel seeds and fry for 1 minute. Add the spinach and cook, stirring, for 10 minutes. Stir in the dhal and continue to cook for 5–10 minutes. Add more salt if necessary.

Transfer to a warmed serving dish.

Cook's Tip

If liked, the okra can be arranged in a radiating pattern on a serving plate.

Cook's Tip

Dhal Sag, from northern India is usually served with Chapatis (see recipe 221). For an even more filling dish add 225 g/8 oz cubed potatoes before the spinach. Serve with relishes, salads and chutneys.

27 | Kabli Channa

Preparation time
20 minutes, plus
overnight soaking time

Cooking time
about 1¾ hours

Serves 4

Calories
270 per portion

You will need
225 g/8 oz chick peas or Bengal
   gram (see Cook's Tip)
750 ml/1¼ pints water
1 teaspoon salt
2 tablespoons oil or concentrated
   butter
1 onion, chopped
2.5 cm/1 inch cinnamon stick
4 cloves
2 garlic cloves, crushed
2.5 cm/1 inch piece root ginger,
   peeled and chopped
2 green chillies, finely chopped
2 teaspoons ground coriander
150 g/5 oz tomatoes, chopped
1 teaspoon garam masala (see
   Cook's Tip recipe 67)
1 tablespoon chopped fresh
   coriander leaves

Wash the chick peas or gram and soak in the water overnight. Add the salt and simmer until tender. Drain, reserving the water, and set aside.

Heat the oil or butter in a pan, add the onion and fry until golden. Add the cinnamon and cloves and fry for a few seconds, then add the garlic, ginger, chillies and ground coriander and fry for 5 minutes. Add the tomatoes and fry until most of the liquid has evaporated.

Add the cooked gram and cook gently for 5 minutes, then add the reserved water and simmer for 20–25 minutes. Add the garam masala and stir well. Sprinkle with the chopped coriander and serve at once.

Cook's Tip

Pulses form a very important
part of the Indian diet – there
are nearly 60 varieties in India,
kabli channa or Bengal gram
(or chick peas) being one of
the most popular. They are
stocked by most major
supermarkets or can be
purchased from specialist
Indian shops.

28 | Celery Sambar

Preparation time
10 minutes

Cooking time
1¼ hours

Serves 4

Calories
280 per portion

You will need
225 g/8 oz tur dhal (yellow pigeon
   peas), washed and drained
1 teaspoon salt
1 teaspoon turmeric
1.2 litres/2 pints water
½ head celery, cut into 5-cm/
   2-inch lengths
2 tablespoons desiccated coconut
3 tablespoons boiling water
½–1 teaspoon small dried red
   chillies
1 teaspoon ground cumin
2 teaspoons ground coriander
50 g/2 oz tamarind, soaked in
   150 ml/¼ pint water
25 g/1 oz butter
pinch of asafoetida (heeng)
   (optional)
1 teaspoon mustard seeds

Put the dhal, salt, turmeric, water and celery in a pan and bring to the boil, then partially cover the pan and simmer for 1 hour.

Put the coconut and boiling water in a food processor or liquidizer and work for 20 seconds. Add the chillies, cumin and coriander and work until smooth. Stir into the dhal with the strained tamarind water and simmer for 15 minutes.

Heat the butter in a small frying pan, add the asafoetida, if using, and the mustard seeds. When the seeds begin to pop, tip the contents of the pan into the dhal mixture. Serve hot.

Cook's Tip

To keep celery crisp, prepare it
as soon as possible after
purchase. Trim and wash the
sticks, then store in the
refrigerator in a jug of iced
water.

29 | Lentil Coconut Curry

Preparation time
20 minutes

Cooking time
55 minutes

Serves 4

Calories
410 per portion

You will need
40 g/1½ oz butter
3 onions, finely chopped
2 garlic cloves, finely chopped
1 tablespoon grated root ginger
2–4 green chillies, finely chopped
1 teaspoon turmeric
225 g/8 oz moong dhal lentils,
    washed and drained
1.2 litres/2 pints water
salt
50 g/2 oz creamed coconut
juice of 1 lemon
finely sliced green chilli rings to
    garnish

Melt the butter in a large pan, add the onions, garlic, ginger and chillies and fry gently, stirring until soft.

Stir in the turmeric and immediately add the dhal. Fry, stirring for 1 minute. Pour in the water, add salt to taste and bring to the boil, then partially cover the pan and simmer gently for 40 minutes.

Add the coconut and stir until dissolved, then stir in the lemon juice. Taste and adjust the seasoning if necessary, cover the pan and simmer for 10 minutes.

Transfer to a warmed serving dish and garnish with the chilli rings.

30 | Tamatar Aloo

Preparation time
20 minutes

Cooking time
15–20 minutes

Serves 4

Calories
130 per portion

You will need
2 tablespoons oil
½ teaspoon mustard seeds
225 g/8 oz potatoes, peeled and
    cut into small cubes
1 teaspoon turmeric
1 teaspoon chilli powder
2 teaspoons paprika
juice of 1 lemon
1 teaspoon sugar
salt
225 g/8 oz tomatoes, quartered
2 tablespoons finely chopped
    fresh coriander leaves

Heat the oil in a pan, add the mustard seeds and fry until they pop – just a few seconds. Add the potatoes and fry for about 5 minutes. Add the spices, lemon juice, sugar and salt to taste, stir well and cook for 5 minutes.

Add the tomatoes, stir well, then simmer for 5–10 minutes until the potatoes are tender. Sprinkle with chopped coriander leaves to serve.

Cook's Tip

Lentils are eaten every day at every meal by most Indian people. For vegetarians they provide valuable protein and are particularly nutritious eaten with rice or wheat. The recipe above is good with bread or rice, or served with an accompanying vegetable or meat dish.

Cook's Tip

Many Indian dishes use mustard seeds – they are small, round reddish-black seeds. When fried for a few seconds they splutter with the heat and give out a delicious smell.

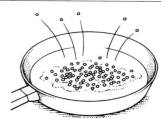

31 | Dhai Aloo

Preparation time
15 minutes

Cooking time
about 25–30 minutes

Serves 4–6

Calories
400–270 per portion

You will need
4 tablespoons oil
1 onion, chopped
2.5 cm/1 inch piece root ginger,
    peeled and finely chopped
1 tablespoon ground coriander
2 green chillies, finely chopped
675 g/1½ lb small new potatoes
1 (227-g/8-oz) can tomatoes
100 g/4 oz raisins
salt
300 ml/½ pint natural yogurt
2 tablespoons chopped fresh
    coriander leaves to garnish

Heat the oil in a large pan, add the onion and ginger and fry until soft. Stir in the ground coriander and chillies and fry for 2 minutes. Add the potatoes, stir well, cover and cook very gently for 5 minutes, stirring occasionally so they colour evenly.

Add the tomatoes with their juice, raisins and salt to taste and stir well. Increase the heat a little and cook, uncovered. As the liquid evaporates, add half the yogurt, a tablespoon at a time. When the potatoes have cooked for 20 minutes and are just about ready, add the remaining yogurt, a tablespoon at a time, lower the heat and cook for 2 minutes.

Sprinkle with the coriander leaves to serve.

32 | Braised Chinese Leaves and Mushrooms

Preparation time
20 minutes

Cooking time
about 5–10 minutes

Serves 4

Calories
180 per portion

You will need
450 g/1 lb Chinese leaves
350 g/12 oz canned straw
    mushrooms or 225 g/8 oz fresh
    straw or button mushrooms
4 tablespoons vegetable oil
2 teaspoons salt
1 teaspoon sugar
1 tablespoon cornflour
3 tablespoons water
50 ml/2 fl oz milk

Separate and wash the Chinese leaves, then cut each leaf in half lengthways. Drain the canned mushrooms; if using fresh, do not peel, simply wash or wipe and then trim off the stalk ends.

Heat about half of the oil in a wok, add the Chinese leaves and stir-fry for 1 minute. Add 1½ teaspoons of the salt and the sugar and stir-fry for a further 1 minute. Remove the Chinese leaves and arrange neatly on a warmed serving dish. Keep hot.

Mix the cornflour to a smooth paste with 3 tablespoons cold water. Heat the remaining oil in the wok until hot, add the mushrooms and remaining salt and stir-fry for 1 minute. Add the cornflour paste and the milk and stir constantly until the sauce is smooth, white and thickened. Pour evenly over the Chinese leaves and serve at once.

Cook's Tip

Ground coriander, not to be confused with green coriander leaves, is a spice with a flavour something like a mixture of sage and lemon peel. It is used extensively in curries and Indian dishes and to give a lift to rice dishes.

Cook's Tip

Chinese straw mushrooms are available both canned and fresh from Chinese supermarkets or stores. Should you have difficulty obtaining them, use small button mushrooms instead.

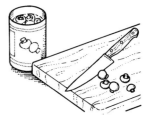

33 | *Vegetables in Tofu Dressing*

Preparation time
20–30 minutes

Cooking time
10–15 minutes

Serves 4

Calories
170 per portion

You will need
3 Chinese dried mushrooms
½ fennel bulb
2 slices boiled ham
1 small carrot, peeled
50 g/2 oz French beans, trimmed
400 ml/14 fl oz Dashi/soup stock
    (see Cook's Tip recipe 235)
1 tablespoon soy sauce
2 teaspoons sugar

For the dressing
100 g/4 oz silken tofu (bean curd)
2 tablespoons tahini
2½ tablespoons sugar
1 teaspoon salt

Soak the mushrooms in warm water for 20–25 minutes, then drain. Squeeze dry, discard the stalks and cut the caps into strips. Cut the fennel, ham, carrots and French beans into strips.

Bring the dashi to the boil in a pan with the soy sauce and sugar. Add the prepared ingredients, except the ham and simmer for 10 minutes. Leave to cool.

To make the dressing, drop the tofu into a pan of boiling water, bring back to the boil, then drain. Place on a board, top with a plate and weight to squeeze out the excess moisture. Force the tofu through a sieve into a bowl. Add the tahini, sugar and·salt and mix well. Drain the cooked vegetables, reserving the juice. Add the vegetables to the dressing with the ham. Mix well, adding a little vegetable juice to thin if necessary. Serve cold.

Cook's Tip

Vegetables are rarely used raw in Japan, but are often part-cooked in a little stock. This combination of vegetables is dressed with a tofu sauce – tofu or bean curd is made from puréed soya beans. It is soft, white and cheese-like and its texture ranges from firm to silken.

34 | *Spicy Fried Okra*

Preparation time
15 minutes

Cooking time
about 15 minutes

Serves 4

Calories
230 per portion

You will need
3 tablespoons ghee
1 large onion, sliced
2 garlic cloves, sliced
1 tablespoon ground coriander
1 teaspoon turmeric
½ teaspoon salt
½ teaspoon freshly ground black pepper
450 g/1 lb okra, trimmed and cut into 1-cm/½-inch pieces
150 ml/¼ pint water
½ teaspoon garam masala (see Cook's Tip recipe 67)

Melt the ghee or butter in a pan, add the onion and garlic and fry until soft. Add the spices and seasonings, except the garam masala and fry for a further 3 minutes, stirring constantly. Add the okra, then stir gently to coat with the spice mixture, taking care not to break them.

Stir in the water and bring to the boil. Lower the heat, cover and simmer for 5–10 minutes until the okra are just tender, but still firm to the bite. Stir in the garam masala and serve hot.

Cook's Tip

Okra are grown throughout the Indian sub-continent – they are small green pods which resemble small gherkins and are sometimes called ladies fingers. They are available canned, but it is better to use them fresh.

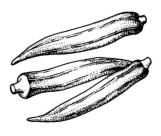

35 | *White-Cooked Cabbage*

Preparation time
10–15 minutes

Cooking time
about 20 minutes

Serves 4

Calories
150 per portion

You will need
1 Savoy or Chinese cabbage, stemmed
300 ml/½ pint stock
1 chicken stock cube
25 g/1 oz lard
1 tablespoon dried shrimps, soaked in hot water for 10 minutes and drained
1 teaspoon sugar
salt and pepper
1½ tablespoons cooked chopped pork or ham

Cut the cabbage lengthways into quarters, then cut each section in half. Bring the stock to the boil in a wok or saucepan. Stir in the stock cube, lard, dried shrimps and sugar. Simmer, stirring, for 2–3 minutes.

Add the cabbage, turning the pieces to ensure they are well coated with the sauce. Bring to the boil, lower the heat and simmer for 4 minutes. Toss the cabbage in the sauce, cover and simmer gently for a further 8–12 minutes.

Transfer the cabbage to a serving dish. Season the sauce with salt and pepper to taste and pour over the cabbage. Sprinkle with pork or ham and serve hot.

36 | *Steamed Chinese Cabbage*

Preparation time
10 minutes

Cooking time
about 35–40 minutes

Serves 4–6

Calories
180–120 per portion

You will need
675 g/1½ lb Chinese cabbage
225 g/8 oz cooked ham
2 tablespoons oil
4 tablespoons chopped spring onions
1 teaspoon salt
2 teaspoons cornflour dissolved in 2 teaspoons water

Discard the tough outer leaves of the cabbage, separate the stalks, wash and cut into 10×15 cm/4×6 inch pieces. Cut the ham into pieces the same size as the cabbage.

Heat the oil in a pan, add the cabbage and stir-fry lightly. Remove from the heat. Lightly oil a heatproof bowl, then sprinkle in the spring onions. Arrange the cabbage and ham in alternate layers in the bowl. Add the salt, cover and steam over a high heat for 30 minutes.

Drain the juice from the bowl into a pan. Add the cornflour mixture and simmer, stirring, until the sauce has thickened. Arrange the ham, cabbage and spring onions on a serving plate. Pour the sauce over and serve hot.

Cook's Tip

White-cooking is a method of cooking in Chinese cuisine that is frequently used for cooking vegetables, particularly leafy vegetables such as cabbage and spinach. Serve white-cooked cabbage with a soy sauce dip if liked.

Cook's Tip

Chinese cabbage, also known as Chinese leaf, Nappa cabbage and celery cabbage looks like a cross between a romaine lettuce and celery. It forms an erect, nearly cylindrical head which is white at the base and pale green at the top. It is very tender and delicate in flavour, and available all year round from supermarkets and Chinese stores.

37 | Aubergines in Fragrant Sauce

Preparation time
20 minutes

Cooking time
5–10 minutes

Serves 4

Calories
220 per portion

You will need
225 g/8 oz aubergines
100 g/4 oz pork fillet
2 spring onions
1 slice root ginger, peeled
1 garlic clove, peeled
600 ml/1 pint oil for deep frying
1 tablespoon soy sauce
1 tablespoon dry sherry
2 teaspoons chilli purée
2 tablespoons cornflour

Peel the aubergines then cut into strips about the size of potato chips. Cut the pork into thin shreds and finely chop the spring onions, ginger and garlic.

Heat the oil in a wok or deep frying pan and deep fry the aubergines for 1–2 mintues. Remove and drain.

Pour off the excess oil, leaving about 1 tablespoon and quickly stir-fry the spring onions, ginger and garlic, then the pork. Add the soy sauce, sherry and chilli purée, blending well. Add the aubergines and cook for 1–2 minutes.

Mix the cornflour with a little water and stir into the mixture. Cook, stirring, until just thickened. Serve hot.

38 | Stir-Fried Lettuce with Oyster Sauce

Preparation time
10 minutes

Cooking time
1 minute

Serves 4

Calories
80 per portion

You will need
2 Cos lettuces
2 tablespoons oil
2 garlic cloves, crushed
2 teaspoons dry sherry
1 teaspoon salt
½ teaspoon sugar
2 tablespoons oyster sauce or soy sauce

Separate the lettuce into leaves and break into 5-cm/2-inch pieces.

Heat the oil in a pan and add the garlic, sherry, salt, sugar and then the lettuce leaves. Cover and cook for 1 minute.

Drain the lettuce and arrange on a serving dish. Pour the oyster sauce on top of the lettuce and serve hot as a main dish, or cold as a salad.

Cook's Tip

The Chinese eat more vegetables than they do meat or poultry and, apart from a few exceptions, most meat, fish or poultry dishes will include some vegetables. It is important to use very fresh vegetables and to prepare just before cooking so that vitamins and minerals are not lost through evaporation.

Cook's Tip

Broccoli or Chinese cabbage may be used instead of the cos lettuce in the above recipe if liked.

39 | *Braised Bamboo Shoots*

Preparation time
10–15 minutes

Cooking time
3–5 minutes

Serves 4

Calories
150 per portion

You will need
4–5 Chinese dried mushrooms
275 g/10 oz bamboo shoots
2 spring onions
3 tablespoons oil
1 tablespoon dry sherry
1 tablespoon soy sauce
2 teaspoons cornflour
50 g/2 oz ham, finely chopped, to garnish

Soak the mushrooms in warm water for 10–15 minutes, squeeze dry and discard the hard stalks, then cut each into 4–5 slices. Cut the bamboo shoots into strips the size of potato chips. Finely chop the spring onions.

Heat the oil in a wok or deep frying pan, add the spring onions, mushrooms and bamboo shoots and stir-fry for about 1 minute, then add the sherry and soy sauce. Continue to cook for a further 1 minute, adding a little stock or water if necessary.

Mix the cornflour with a little cold water, add to the mixture and stir until the juice thickens. Serve at once, garnished with the chopped ham.

40 | *Palak Aloo*

Preparation time
10 minutes

Cooking time
15–20 minutes

Serves 4

Calories
180 per portion (300 with additional ghee)

You will need
40 g/1½ oz ghee or butter
225 g/8 oz potatoes, peeled and cut into chunks
2 teaspoons garlic paste
2 teaspoons ginger paste
1 green chilli, halved and seeded
450 g/1 lb spinach, roughly chopped
1 tablespoon chopped fresh coriander leaves
salt
50 g/2 oz melted butter or ghee for serving (optional)

Heat the ghee or butter in a pan and fry the potatoes for 4–5 minutes. Add the garlic and ginger pastes and the chilli. Fry for 1–2 minutes.

Stir in the spinach, coriander and salt to taste. Add a little water and continue frying for 10–15 minutes until the potatoes are tender and the spinach is dry.

Serve hot, with melted butter or ghee poured over the top if liked.

Cook's Tip

Fresh bamboo shoots are very hard to find and are generally only available canned. Drain well before use. In China, Japan and India they are eaten fresh, like asparagus. Once the can of bamboo shoots is opened, the shoots may be kept immersed in water in a covered jar for up to 1 week in the refrigerator.

Cook's Tip

If liked, frozen chopped spinach can be used in the above recipe. You will need 225 g/8 oz which must be thawed and squeezed dry in a fine sieve before use.

41 | *Vegetable Curry*

Preparation time
15 minutes

Cooking time
20–25 minutes

Serves 4

Calories
100 per portion

You will need
25–40 g/1–1½ oz ghee or 2–3
  tablespoons oil
1 small onion, chopped
450 g/1 lb diced mixed vegetables
  (potatoes, carrots, swede,
  peas, beans or cauliflower, for
  example)
about 1 teaspoon chilli powder
2 teaspoons ground coriander
½ teaspoon turmeric
salt
2–3 tomatoes, skinned and
  chopped

Heat the ghee or oil in a pan and gently fry the onion until light brown. Add the diced vegetables and stir in the chilli powder, coriander, turmeric and salt to taste. Fry for 2–3 minutes.

Add the tomatoes, stir well and add 1–2 tablespoons water, then cover and cook gently for 10–12 minutes until the mixture is dry.

Serve as a side dish or as a main dish with rice or naan bread (see recipe 219).

42 | *Pumpkin Curry*

Preparation time
25 minutes

Cooking time
about 30 minutes

Serves 4

Calories
220 per portion

You will need
450 g/1 lb pumpkin
20 g/¾ oz tamarind pods
40 g/1½ oz ghee or 3 tablespoons
  oil
¼ teaspoon cumin seeds
¼ teaspoon mustard seeds
¼ teaspoon fenugreek seeds
¼ teaspoon onion seeds
¼ teaspoon aniseed
3 medium potatoes, peeled and
  cut into chunks
about 1 teaspoon chilli powder
½ teaspoon ground turmeric
1 teaspoon ground coriander
salt
1 teaspoon sugar

Peel the pumpkin in alternate strips so as to keep the flesh intact during cooking and cut into cubes. Wash and drain well.

Soak the tamarind pods in a cup of hot water for 10–15 minutes and extract the pulp. Repeat the process to extract any remaining pulp.

Heat the ghee or oil in a pan and fry the cumin, mustard seeds, fenugreek, onion seeds and aniseed for 30 seconds, then add the potatoes and fry for 2–3 minutes. Add the pumpkin cubes, stir well and fry for 4–5 minutes.

Stir in the chilli, turmeric, coriander, salt to taste and sugar, and continue frying for 5–6 minutes. Add the tamarind pulp, cover and cook until the potatoes are tender. Serve hot.

Cook's Tip

This is the dry method for cooking a curried mixture – just a little water being added to prevent the vegetables from sticking to the pan. If a moister curry is preferred then 30 ml/½ pint water may be added with the tomatoes and simmered for 5–6 minutes until tender.

Cook's Tip

Pumpkins shouldn't be reserved for Halloweeen lanterns. A nutritious vegetable, high in vitamin A, it is delicious roasted in the oven or boiled and masked with lots of black pepper and nutmeg.

43 | *Dry Turnip Curry*

Preparation time
10 minutes

Cooking time
about 20 minutes

Serves 4

Calories
200 per portion

You will need
450 g/1 lb turnips, peeled
50 g/2 oz ghee or 75 g/3 oz
  butter
1 onion, sliced
1 green chilli, seeded and finely
  chopped
1 teaspoon garam masala (see
  Cook's Tip recipe 67)
salt
about ¼ teaspoon sugar (optional)
juice of 1 lemon

Slice the turnips into rounds and cook in 50 ml/2 fl oz boiling water until tender and dry.

Heat the ghee or butter in a pan and fry the onion until light brown. Add the chilli, turnips, garam masala and salt to taste. Taste and add the sugar if liked. Cook for about 5 minutes.

Serve hot as a side dish, sprinkled with lemon juice.

44 | *Gobhi Masala*

Preparation time
20 minutes

Cooking time
about 30 minutes

Serves 4

Calories
220 per portion

You will need
1 large cauliflower
1 bay leaf
4 cardamoms
1 clove
1 cinnamon stick
1 tablespoon mustard seeds
2 tablespoons poppy seeds
2 onions, chopped
50 g/2 oz root ginger, grated
2 garlic cloves, crushed
½ teaspoon turmeric
3 tablespoons tomato purée
50 g/2 oz butter
4 green chillies, chopped
450 g/1 lb tomatoes, peeled
300 ml/½ pint natural yogurt

Divide the cauliflower into florets and steam for 15 minutes.

Place the bay leaf, cardamoms, clove, cinnamon, mustard and poppy seeds in a small pan and roast over a low heat until they give off a strong aroma. Cool slightly, then grind to a powder. Add half the onion, ginger and garlic and work to a smooth paste. Mix in the turmeric.

Mix the tomato purée with 150 ml/¼ pint water and set aside. Melt the butter in a wok or deep frying pan. Add the remaining chopped onions and chillies and cook until soft. Add the paste and cook, stirring, for 5 minutes.

Quarter the tomatoes and add to the tomato liquid. Bring to the boil and simmer for 5 minutes. Stir in the yogurt and cauliflower and coat thoroughly. Cover and simmer gently for 15 minutes.

Cook's Tip

The above recipe can also be
used to cook other root
vegetables like swede and
carrots.

Cook's Tip

Take care when roasting the
spices in the frying pan that
they do not overcook or they
will taste very bitter when
ground.

45 | *Aviyal*

Preparation time
20 minutes

Cooking time
about 20 minutes

Serves 4–6

Calories
650–430 per portion

You will need
flesh and liquid from 1 coconut
300 ml/½ pint boiling water
175 g/6 oz ghee
2 large onions, thinly sliced
6 garlic cloves, thinly sliced
100 g/4 oz root ginger, peeled and
  thinly sliced
4 green chillies, seeded and
  chopped
1 teaspoon mustard seeds
1 teaspoon sesame seeds
2 teaspoons onion seeds
2 teaspoons turmeric
100 g/4 oz canned tomatoes
225 g/8 oz courgettes, sliced
100 g/4 oz French beans, trimmed
2 red peppers, seeded and sliced
100 g/4 oz carrots, cut into sticks
1 tablespoon garam masala

Slice half of the coconut flesh thinly and set aside. Grate the remainder into a liquidizer, add the coconut liquid and blend. Place in bowl, pour over the boiling water.

Heat the ghee in a pan, add the onions and garlic until softened. Add the ginger and chillies and cook for 1 minute. Stir in the mustard, sesame, onion seeds and turmeric and cook for 2 minutes. Strain in the coconut liquid, bring to the boil, add the canned tomatoes and vegetables. Return to the boil, cover and simmer for 5–10 minutes. Sprinkle in the garam masala and add the sliced coconut. Cook for 2 minutes then serve hot, garnished with chopped coriander if liked.

Cook's Tip

To crack open a coconut put it in the oven at 150 C/30 F gas mark 2 for 25 minutes, placed in a container to catch any drips. It should crack by itself while cooking.

46 | *Courgette Curry*

Preparation time
15 minutes

Cooking time
about 15 minutes

Serves 4

Calories
600 per portion

You will need
juice of 1 lemon
675 g/1½ lb courgettes, sliced
100 g/4 oz desiccated coconut
150 ml/¼ pint boiling water
175 g/6 oz ghee
1 large onion, sliced
2 garlic cloves, sliced
1 teaspoon mustard seeds
1 teaspoon onion seeds
1–2 teaspoons chilli powder
1 teaspoon freshly ground black
  pepper
1 teaspoon turmeric
100 g/4 oz canned tomatoes
1½ teaspoons salt
2 teaspoons garam masala (see
  Cook's Tip recipe 67)

Pour the lemon juice over the courgettes and set aside. Immerse the coconut in the boiling water and leave for 5 minutes.

Heat the ghee in a pan, add the onion and garlic and fry gently until golden. Mix in the mustard and onion seeds and fry for 1 minute. Add the chilli powder to taste, pepper and turmeric and stir for 30 seconds. Add the courgettes and lemon juice, stir well, then add the tomatoes and salt. Bring to the boil, reduce the heat and simmer for 5 minutes, then add the garam masala. Cook for a few minutes until the courgettes are tender, then serve.

Cook's Tip

This is a variation on a medium-hot dish traditionally made in central India. It makes a good accompaniment to a lamb curry.

47 | Stuffed Aubergines

Preparation time
15 minutes

Cooking time
15–20 minutes

Serves 4

Calories
160 per portion

You will need
8 small aubergines
2 tablespoons ground coriander
1 tablespoon ground cumin
1 teaspoon garam masala (see Cook's Tip recipe 67)
2 teaspoons mango powder
salt
chilli powder
2–3 tablespoons oil
2 small onions, quartered

Carefully slit the aubergines lengthways into 4 sections, held together at the stalk end. Mix all the ground spices and mango powder with salt and chilli powder to taste and carefully stuff some of the mixture into each of the aubergines, pressing the sections back together.

Heat the oil in a large frying pan, add the aubergines and onion quarters and fry over a gentle heat, turning carefully once or twice, until tender. Serve hot or cold.

48 | Stir-Fried Summer Vegetables

Preparation time
20 minutes

Cooking time
about 5 minutes

Serves 4–6

Calories
140–90 per portion

You will need
2 tablespoons oil
2 spring onions, sliced
2.5 cm/1 inch piece root ginger, peeled and sliced
2 garlic cloves, sliced
2 chillies, seeded and chopped
50 g/2 oz button mushrooms
100 g/4 oz baby carrots, peeled
100 g/4 oz mangetout, trimmed
100 g/4 oz French beans, trimmed
50 g/2 oz beansprouts
1 red pepper, cored, seeded and sliced
2 celery sticks, sliced
few cauliflower florets
4 tablespoons light soy sauce
2 tablespoons dry sherry
1 teaspoon sesame oil

Heat the oil in a wok, add the spring onions, ginger and garlic and stir-fry for 30 seconds. Add the chillies and all the vegetables. Toss well and cook, stirring for 2 minutes. Stir in the soy sauce and sherry and cook for 2 minutes.

Sprinkle over the sesame oil, pile into a warmed serving dish and serve at once.

Cook's Tip

Cover the pan if the oil starts to splutter during cooking – but remember to keep the heat low to ensure a good tender result.

Cook's Tip

Many Chinese dishes are cooked in a wok and if you plan to cook this type of cuisine frequently then it is well worth buying one. You can, however, use a deep frying pan with fairly straight sides just as well.

49 | *Indian Vegetable Medley*

Preparation time
15 minutes

Cooking time
about 40 minutes

Serves 4–6

Calories
200–130 per portion

You will need
3 tablespoons oil
1 teaspoon fennel seeds
2 onions, sliced
1 teaspoon ground coriander
1 teaspoon cumin seeds
1 teaspoon chilli powder
2 teaspoons chopped root ginger
2 garlic cloves, crushed
1 small aubergine, thinly sliced
1 potato, peeled and cubed
1 green pepper, cored, seeded and sliced
2 courgettes, sliced
1 (400-g/14-oz) can tomatoes
2 green chillies, chopped
salt
50 g/2 oz frozen peas

Heat the oil, stir in the fennel seeds and cook for 1 minute, stirring constantly. Add the onions and cook for 5 minutes until pale brown. Lower the heat, add all the spices and cook, stirring, for 1 minute. Add the ginger, garlic, aubergine and potato, mix well and cook for 15 minutes.

Add the green pepper, courgettes, tomatoes with their juice, chillies and salt to taste. Bring slowly to the boil, then simmer, stirring occasionally for 10 minutes.

Stir in the peas and cook for 3 minutes. Transfer to a warmed serving dish and serve at once.

50 | *Stir-Fried Garlic Spinach*

Preparation time
4–5 minutes

Cooking time
5–6 minutes

Serves 4

Calories
120 per portion

You will need
1 kg/2 lb spinach
2 tablespoons oil
4 spring onions, chopped
1 teaspoon light soy sauce
pinch of sugar
pinch of salt
2 garlic cloves, crushed
1 teaspoon toasted sesame seeds

Wash the spinach thoroughly and remove all the stems. Drain thoroughly.

Heat the oil in a wok or frying pan, add the spring onions and fry for 30 seconds. Add the spinach and stir-fry for about 2 minutes, until the leaves are coated in the oil and have wilted. Add the soy sauce, sugar, salt and garlic and continue stir-frying for 3 minutes. Pour off any excess liquid.

Transfer to a warmed serving dish and sprinkle with the sesame seeds to serve.

Cook's Tip

Indian spices impart a marvellous flavour to meats, fish and vegetables. Buy spices whole and grind them yourself as required, to ensure optimum flavour and aroma.

Cook's Tip

Garlic is one of the most versatile aromatics with a pungent power of flavouring and enhancing many foods. Its character and flavour change when cooked: if it is very slowly stewed it develops a mild sweetness in the dish; if it is fried to a nutty brown it becomes more pungent with quite a bite.

51 | *Stir-Fried Spiced Cucumber*

Preparation time
25 minutes, including
salting time

Cooking time
5 minutes

Serves 4

Calories
90 per portion

You will need
1½ cucumbers
2 teaspoons salt
1 tablespoon oil
¼ teaspoon chilli bean sauce or
  chilli powder
6 garlic cloves, crushed
1½ tablespoons black beans,
  coarsely chopped
5 tablespoons chicken stock
1 teaspoon sesame oil
cucumber slices to garnish

Peel the cucumbers, slice in half lengthways, remove the seeds, then cube. Sprinkle with salt and leave to drain for about 20 minutes. Rinse, drain and dry.

Heat the oil in a wok or frying pan and when it is almost smoking, add the chilli bean sauce or powder, garlic and black beans and stir-fry for 30 seconds. Add the cucumber and toss well for about 3 seconds to coat in the spices. Add the stock and continue stir-frying over a high heat for 3–4 minutes until almost all the liquid has evaporated and the cucumber is tender.

Transfer to a warmed serving dish, sprinkle with the sesame oil and garnish with cucumber slices, serving at once.

52 | *Stir-Fried Mushrooms*

Preparation time
20 minutes

Cooking time
12 minutes

Serves 4–6

Calories
75–45 per portion

You will need
50 g/2 oz small Chinese dried
  mushrooms
1 tablespoon oil
1 teaspoon finely chopped root
  ginger
2 spring onions, finely chopped
1 garlic clove, crushed
225 g/8 oz button mushrooms
1 (227-g/8-oz) can straw
  mushrooms, drained
1 teaspoon chilli bean sauce or
  chilli powder
2 teaspoons sake (rice wine) or
  dry sherry
2 teaspoons dark soy sauce
1 tablespoon chicken stock
pinch of sugar
pinch of salt
1 teaspoon sesame oil
fresh coriander leaves to garnish

Soak the dried mushrooms in warm water for 15 minutes. Drain and squeeze dry, discard the hard stalks.

Heat the oil in a wok or deep frying pan, add the ginger, spring onions and garlic and stir-fry for 5 seconds. Stir in the dried and button mushrooms and cook, stirring, for 5 minutes.

Stir in the remaining ingredients, mixing well, and stir-fry for a further 5 minutes. Transfer to a warmed serving dish and garnish with coriander leaves.

Cook's Tip

The above recipe uses salted black beans – these are soya beans which have been steamed, spiced and preserved in salt. They are sold in cans or packets and will keep for up to 1 year.

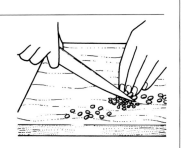

Cook's Tip

Sake, or rice wine, is a popular Chinese drink made from rice, millet and spring water. Its unique flavour is attributed to the special yeast used. It is available from Chinese and oriental supermarkets; dry sherry can be used instead.

57 | *Crispy Vegetables*

Preparation time
15 minutes

Cooking time
20 minutes

Serves 6

Calories
230 per portion

You will need
100 g/4 oz plain flour
pinch of salt
1 tablespoon oil
150 ml/¼ pint water
2 egg whites, stiffly whisked
450 g/1 lb mixed vegetables
 (cauliflower florets, beans,
 whole mushrooms, mangetout,
 pepper strips, aubergine cubes
 are all suitable)
oil for deep frying

Sift the flour and salt into a bowl, gradually beat in the oil and water, then fold in the egg white.

Heat the oil in a wok or frying pan, dip the vegetables into the batter, then deep-fry, in batches, for 2–3 minutes until golden.

Drain and serve with a dip (see Cook's Tip).

58 | *Potato and Courgette*

Preparation time
15 minutes

Cooking time
25 minutes

Serves 4

Calories
160 per portion

You will need
3 tablespoons oil
1 large garlic clove, crushed
½ teaspoon chilli powder
2 teaspoons ground coriander
1 teaspoon ground cumin
1 teaspoon salt
2 tablespoons water
450 g/1 lb courgettes, sliced
225 g/8 oz new potatoes, halved
1 tablespoon finely sliced red
 pepper to garnish

Heat the oil in a pan and fry the garlic for 30 seconds. Add the spices, salt and water, stir well and fry gently for 2 minutes. Add the vegetables, stir thoroughly, cover the pan and cook gently for 20 minutes or until the vegetables are cooked, stirring occasionally.

Garnish with the red pepper to serve.

Cook's Tip

To make a tasty dip for this recipe put 1–2 chopped garlic cloves, 4 tomatoes, skinned, seeded and chopped, 1 teaspoon chilli powder, 2 avocado pears, peeled and stoned, 1 tablespoon chopped fresh coriander and a pinch of ground coriander in a blender and work until smooth. Spoon into a serving dish and chill.

Cook's Tip

To crush garlic without a crusher, place a peeled garlic clove on a chopping board and sprinkle with a little salt. Then crush with the flat, wide blade of a knife, pressing hard with the palm of your hand.

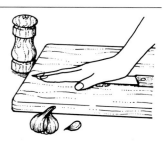

59 | *Cabbage Foogath*

Preparation time
15 minutes

Cooking time
15 minutes

Serves 4

Calories
140 per portion

You will need
2 tablespoons oil
1 large onion, finely minced
2.5 cm/1 inch piece root ginger,
    peeled and finely chopped
3 green chillies, sliced
1 garlic clove, crushed
450 g/1 lb green cabbage,
    shredded
25 g/1 oz freshly grated coconut
100 g/4 oz peeled prawns

Heat the oil in a wok or deep frying pan, add the onion, ginger, chillies and garlic and fry until beginning to colour. Stir in the cabbage and continue frying for 5 minutes. Add the coconut and cook, stirring, for 2 minutes. Add the prawns and simmer for 2 minutes.

Transfer to a warmed serving dish and serve at once.

60 | *Sri Lankan Curry*

Preparation time
25 minutes

Cooking time
40 minutes

Serves 4

Calories
250 per portion

You will need
2 onions, thinly sliced
2 garlic cloves, finely chopped
1 tablespoon grated root ginger
4 green chillies, 2 finely chopped
    and 2 slit
1 teaspoon powdered lemon grass
1 teaspoon turmeric
salt
6 curry leaves
600 ml/1 pint thin coconut milk
    (see Cook's Tip recipe 2)
225 g/8 oz each courgettes,
    potatoes, peppers and carrots,
    sliced
300 ml/½ pint thick coconut milk
    (see Cook's Tip recipe 3)

Put the onions, garlic, ginger, chopped chillies, lemon grass, turmeric, salt, curry leaves and thin coconut milk in a pan. Bring to simmering point and cook gently, un-covered, for 20 minutes.

Add the vegetables, slit chillies and thick coconut milk and cook for a further 20 minutes or until the vegetables are tender.

Transfer to a warmed serving dish to serve.

Cook's Tip

When buying a coconut, choose one that is heavy for its size. To open it, pierce the 'eyes' with a skewer and pour away the liquid. Put the coconut in a preheated moderately hot oven, 190 C, 375 F, gas 5, for 15 minutes.

Give it a sharp tap with a hammer or mallet and it will break open. Using a sharp knife, prise away the flesh from the shell, then peel off the brown skin and cut the flesh into pieces.

Cook's Tip

Sri Lankan curry can be made with other vegetables – try it with peas, beans and aubergine for example.

61 | Brinjal and Potato Curry

Preparation time
25 minutes

Cooking time
30 minutes

Serves 4

Calories
180 per portion

You will need
350 g/12 oz aubergine, cubed
2 teaspoons salt
3 tablespoons oil
1–2 teaspoons chilli powder
1 teaspoon turmeric
2 teaspoons ground cumin
2 teaspoons ground coriander
2.5 cm/1 inch piece root ginger, peeled and finely chopped
350 g/12 oz potatoes, peeled and cubed
1 (227-g/8-oz) can tomatoes, sieved
juice of 1 lemon
2 tablespoons chopped fresh coriander leaves
1 teaspoon garam masala (see Cook's Tip recipe 67)
lime slices to garnish

Sprinkle the aubergine with 1 teaspoon of the salt, place in a colander and set aside for 20 minutes.

Heat the oil in a pan, add the chilli powder, turmeric, cumin, ground coriander and ginger and fry for 2 minutes. Add the potatoes and drained aubergine and fry, stirring for 2 minutes.

Add the tomatoes, lemon juice, chopped coriander and remaining salt. Cover and simmer for 25 minutes or until the vegetables are tender. Just before serving stir in the garam masala. Garnish with lime slices to serve.

62 | Vegetable Biryani

Preparation time
35 minutes, including soaking time

Cooking time
1 hour

Oven temperature
180 C, 350 F, gas 4

Serves 4–6

Calories
580–380 per portion

You will need
450 g/1 lb Basmati rice, washed, soaked and drained (see recipe 207)
salt
3 tablespoons oil
5 cm/2 inch cinnamon stick
6 cardamoms
6 cloves
2 onions, sliced
2 garlic cloves, finely sliced
2 green chillies, finely sliced
1 tablespoon grated root ginger
1 kg/2 lb mixed vegetables, cut in pieces
1 (400-g/14-oz) can tomatoes

Par-boil the rice in plenty of boiling salted water for 3 minutes, then drain.

Heat the oil in a large pan and fry the cinnamon, cardamoms and cloves for a few seconds. Add the onions, garlic, chillies and ginger and fry until soft and golden. Add the vegetables and fry for 2–3 minutes. Add the tomatoes, with their juice, and salt to taste. Cover and simmer for 20 minutes or until the vegetables are tender.

Layer the vegetables and rice in a casserole, starting and finishing with vegetables. Cover tightly and bake for 25–30 minutes until the rice is tender. Serve at once.

Cook's Tip

Brinjal and Potato Curry is an example of a curry made with a combination of vegetables. Potato is a popular ingredient because it absorbs the spices and juices. If the sauce starts to dry out too much during the latter stage of cooking, add a little water to prevent burning. It is delicious with Puri (see recipe 220).

Cook's Tip

If you have a food processor then simply rough-chop all the vegetables using the knife attachment. Take care not to over-process the ingredients so that they become too fine.

63 | *Stuffed Bhindi*

Preparation time
30 minutes, plus 12
hours marinating time

Serves 4

Calories
40 per portion

You will need
450 g/1 lb tender okra
10 garlic cloves, finely chopped
6 green chillies, finely chopped
7.5 cm/3 inch piece root ginger,
   peeled and finely chopped
4 tablespoons finely chopped
   fresh mint
1 teaspoon salt
600 ml/1 pint red wine vinegar
sugar
mint leaves to garnish

Top and tail the okra and slit them down one side.

Mix the garlic, chillies, ginger, mint and salt together thoroughly. Stuff the okra with this mixture and arrange in layers in a dish. Sweeten the vinegar to taste with sugar and pour over the okra to cover.

Cover and leave in a cool place for 12–24 hours for the flavours to mingle. Serve chilled with mint leaves.

64 | *Stir-Fried Vegetable Omelette*

Preparation time
5 minutes

Cooking time
10 minutes

Serves 4–6

Calories
230–150 per portion

You will need
1 tablespoon oil
1 onion, finely chopped
1 garlic clove, crushed
2 potatoes, peeled, quartered and
   finely sliced
½ green or red pepper, cored,
   seeded and finely chopped
handful of broccoli florets
3 tomatoes, sliced
¼ cucumber, chopped
5–6 large eggs, beaten
1 heaped teaspoon chopped fresh
   parsley
½ teaspoon dried mixed herbs
pepper

Heat the oil in a large frying pan, add the onion and fry, stirring until softened. Stir in the garlic, potatoes, pepper and broccoli and cook, stirring and turning for about 6–7 minutes, until softened but still crisp – add a little water if they start to stick. Add the tomatoes and cucumber, stir well then spread the mixture out flat.

Pour over the eggs and stir to distribute. Cook until the eggs begin to set, then place under a preheated hot grill until the top has set.

Cut into wedges and sprinkle with the parsley, mixed herbs and pepper. Serve at once.

Cook's Tip

Stuffed Bhindi depends for its success on tender young okra – and you really have to like garlic to enjoy it! In Bombay it is served with plain fried fish or chicken or with a dry curry.

Cook's Tip

Always be careful not to overcook egg dishes. Remove them from the heat just before they are cooked and the heat of the pan will finish them off. Serve the omelette with wholemeal rolls if liked.

65 | Stuffed Cabbage Leaves

Preparation time
20 minutes

Cooking time
35 minutes

Serves 4–6

Calories
510–340 per portion

You will need
1 cabbage
5 tablespoons oil
1 onion, chopped
1 cm/½ inch piece root ginger,
    peeled and chopped
1 teaspoon turmeric
450 g/1 lb lean minced lamb
75 g/3 oz long-grain rice
2 tomatoes, skinned and chopped
grated rind and juice of 2 lemons
2 teaspoons sugar
salt and pepper
150 ml/¼ pint water

Hollow out the stem end of the cabbage and discard. Place the cabbage in a large pan, cover with water and bring to the boil. Remove from the heat, cover and leave for 15 minutes; drain.

Fry the onion in 2 tablespoons of the oil until soft. Add the ginger and turmeric and fry for 1 minute. Add the lamb and fry briefly until brown. Cool slightly, then mix with the remaining ingredients, minus the water.

Carefully remove 12 inner leaves of the cabbage. Divide the meat mixture between these, gently squeezing out and reserving any liquid. Shape each leaf into a packet. Heat the remaining oil in a large frying pan, add the cabbage rolls in one layer and heat through. Pour over the reserved liquid and water. Cover and simmer for about 30 minutes, uncover, turn over and cook for a further 5 minutes. Serve hot.

Cook's Tip

Most of the liquid should have evaporated from the dish towards the end of cooking – if it hasn't then increase the heat and cook uncovered for a few minutes longer.

66 | Spicy Turnips

Preparation time
20 minutes

Cooking time
about 20 minutes

Serves 4–6

Calories
260–180 per portion

You will need
about 3 tablespoons ghee or
    concentrated butter
1 kg/2 lb turnips, peeled and
    quartered
2 garlic cloves, peeled
2 green chillies
2.5 cm/1 inch piece root ginger,
    peeled
1 teaspoon cumin seeds
2 teaspoons coriander seeds
2 tablespoons natural yogurt
1 teaspoon salt
150 ml/¼ pint water
1 teaspoon sugar
1 teaspoon garam masala (see
    Cook's Tip recipe 67)

Heat the ghee in a pan, add the turnips and fry lightly then set aside.

Put the garlic, chillies, ginger, cumin, coriander and yogurt into a liquidizer or food processor and work to a paste. Add to the pan and fry for 2 minutes.

Return the turnips to the pan, add the salt and stir well. Add the water and simmer, covered, for about 10 minutes, until almost tender. Uncover the pan, add the sugar and garam masala and cook briskly, stirring until most of the liquid has evaporated.

Cook's Tip

This is a deliciously spicy vegetable side dish to serve with a meat or poultry main course. You could of course use swede instead of the turnips if liked.

67 | *Masoor Dhal*

Preparation time
15 minutes

Cooking time
about 35 minutes

Serves 4

Calories
350 per portion

You will need
4 tablespoons oil
6 cloves
6 cardamoms
2.5 cm/1 inch cinnamon stick
1 onion, chopped
2.5 cm/1 inch piece ginger, chopped
1 green chilli, finely chopped
1 garlic clove, chopped
½ teaspoon garam masala (see Cook's Tip)
225 g/8 oz masoor dhal or orange lentils
salt
juice of 1 lemon

Heat the oil in a pan, add the cloves, cardamoms and cinnamon and fry until they start to swell. Add the onion and fry until softened. Add the ginger, chilli, garlic and garam masala and cook for about 5 minutes.

Add the lentils, stir thoroughly and fry for 1 minute. Add salt to taste and enough water to come about 3 cm/1¼ inches above the level of the lentils. Bring to the boil, cover and simmer for about 20 minutes, until really thick and tender.

Sprinkle with the lemon juice, stir and serve at once.

68 | *Spicy Vegetables*

Preparation time
30 minutes, including soaking time

Cooking time
about 15 minutes

Serves 4

Calories
360 per portion

You will need
1.2 litres/2 pints water
200 g/7 oz bean threads
3 tablespoons vegetable oil
225 g/8 oz Chinese cabbage, shredded
salt
1 large carrot, thinly sliced
100 g/4 oz fresh spinach leaves, cooked and chopped
8 medium dried Chinese mushrooms, soaked in warm water for 20 minutes then drained

For the sauce
1 tablespoon sesame oil
1 tablespoon soy sauce
2 teaspoons sugar
2 teaspoons sesame seeds
½ teaspoon salt

Bring the water to the boil in a pan, add the bean threads and boil for 3 minutes. Drain and set aside.

Heat 2 tablespoons of the oil in a pan, add the cabbage and salt to taste and fry for 2 minutes. Remove and set aside. Heat the remaining oil in the pan, add the carrot and fry for 1 minute. Return the cabbage to the pan, add the spinach and mushrooms and cook for 2 minutes, stirring constantly.

To make the sauce, put all the ingredients in a pan and stir well. Bring to the boil then mix into the vegetable mixture with the bean threads. Heat through to serve.

Cook's Tip

Garam masala is a ground spice mixture used in many Indian recipes. You can buy it or prepare your own: the flavour is better when it is freshly ground. To make it, place 2 tablespoons black peppercorns, 1 tablespoon **black cumin seeds, 1 small cinnamon stick, 1 teaspoon cloves, ¼ nutmeg, 2 teaspoons cardamom seeds and 2 tablespoons coriander seeds in a coffee grinder or pestle and mortar and grind to a powder. Store in a jar.**

Cook's Tip

Bean threads are also known as cellophane noodles. They are very fine dried noodles made from moong bean flour and are sold in packets. Soak in water for about 10 minutes before using.

Fish and Seafood Dishes

Here are many of the old oriental favourites and classics, like sashimi, paper-wrapped fish and spicy prawns alongside a good selection of not so well known dishes that are sure to become family favourites, like crab in black bean sauce, sole with saté sauce and stir-fried squid with mixed vegetables.

69 | Grilled Spiced Fish

(Illustrated on front jacket)

Preparation time
10 minutes, plus 2 hours marinating time

Cooking time
6–8 minutes

Serves 4

Calories
220 per portion

You will need
2 large or 4 small plaice, cleaned
150 g/5 oz pint natural yogurt
2 garlic cloves, crushed
1 teaspoon ground coriander seeds
½ teaspoon chilli powder
1 teaspoon garam masala (see Cook's Tip recipe 67)
1 tablespoon vinegar
1 tablespoon oil
salt

Slash the fish on both sides and place in separate shallow dishes. Mix the remaining ingredients together adding salt to taste, and divide between the fish. Spoon it all over one side and leave for 1 hour, then turn and spoon over the juice that has collected in the dish. Leave to marinate for another hour.

Cook under a preheated moderate grill for 3–4 minutes. Turn and baste with any juices collected in the grill pan, then cook for a further 3–4 minutes and serve at once.

70 | Paper-Wrapped Fish

Preparation time
15 minutes

Cooking time
3 minutes

Serves 4

Calories
300 per portion

You will need
4 (100-g/4-oz) plaice or sole fillets
pinch of salt
2 tablespoons dry sherry
1 tablespoon oil
2 tablespoons shredded spring onion
2 tablespoons shredded root ginger
oil for deep frying
spring onion flowers to garnish (see Cook's Tip)

Cut the fish fillets into 2.5-cm/1-inch squares. Sprinkle with the salt and toss in the sherry.

Cut out 15-cm/6-inch squares of greaseproof paper and brush with the oil. Place a piece of fish on each square of paper and arrange some spring onions and ginger on top. Fold into envelopes, tucking in the flaps to secure.

Heat the oil in a wok or deep frier to 180 C/375 F and deep-fry the wrapped fish for 3 minutes. Drain and arrange on a warmed serving dish. Garnish with spring onion flowers and serve at once. Each person unwraps their own parcels with chopsticks.

Cook's Tip

When buying whole fresh fish, look for the following characteristics – bright eyes, red gills, flesh firm to the touch, shiny scales and a mild, pleasant odour.

Cook's Tip

To make spring onion flowers, trim the green top and remove the white part. Carefully shred the top leaving 2.5 cm/1 inch attached at the base. Immerse in iced water until the spring onion opens out and curls.

71 | *Fish Molee*

Preparation time
10 minutes

Cooking time
20–25 minutes

Serves 4

Calories
400 per portion

You will need
675 g/1½ lb cod fillet, skinned and
    cut into 4 pieces
2 tablespoons plain flour
4 tablespoons oil
2 onions, sliced
2 garlic cloves, crushed
1 teaspoon turmeric
4 green chillies, finely chopped
2 tablespoons lemon juice
175 ml/6 fl oz thick coconut milk
    (see Cook's Tip recipe 3)
salt

Coat the fish with the flour. Heat the oil in a frying pan, add the fish and fry quickly on both sides. Remove with a slotted spoon and set aside.

Add the onion and garlic to the pan and fry until soft and golden. Add the turmeric, chillies, lemon juice, coconut milk and salt to taste. Simmer, uncovered for 10 minutes or until thickened.

Add the fish and any juices, spoon over the sauce and cook gently for 2–3 minutes, until tender.

72 | *Trout with Salted Cabbage*

Preparation time
15 minutes

Cooking time
13 minutes

Serves 4

Calories
240 per portion

You will need
2 tablespoons oil
1 onion, chopped
2.5 cm/1 inch piece root ginger,
    peeled and shredded
4 trout, cleaned
150 ml/¼ pint chicken stock (see
    Cook's Tip)
25 g/1 oz pickled cabbage,
    chopped
25 g/1 oz canned bamboo shoots,
    drained and sliced
1 tablespoon soy sauce
2 teaspoons dry sherry

Heat the oil in a wok or deep frying pan, add the onion and ginger and cook for 1 minute. Add the trout and fry for 1 minute on each side, until browned.

Stir in the stock, then add the cabbage, bamboo shoots, soy sauce and sherry. Cook for 10 minutes, basting the fish occasionally.

Transfer to a warmed serving dish and garnish as shown if liked. Serve at once.

Cook's Tip

When buying fish fillets or steaks, look for a fresh cut appearance, firm elastic flesh that does not separate easily from the bones and, of course, a mild, pleasant odour.

Cook's Tip

For home-made chicken stock, break up a carcass and put in a large saucepan with a quartered onion, bayleaf and mace blade. Cover with water and bring to the boil. Simmer for 2–3 hours, then strain.

73 | *Prawns with Tamarind*

Preparation time
10 minutes, plus 1 hour for the tamarind paste

Cooking time
about 10 minutes

Serves 4

Calories
300 per portion

You will need
225 g/8 oz tamarind
100 ml/4 fl oz water
1 small red pepper, cored, seeded and chopped
25 g/1 oz small onions, chopped
2 garlic cloves, chopped
1 red chilli, seeded and chopped
1 tablespoon ground lemon grass
6 tablespoons oil
4 teaspoons caster sugar
2 teaspoons lime juice
salt
450 g/1 lb unpeeled Mediterranean prawns, heads left on and de-veined through the shell

To make the tamarind paste, place the tamarind and water in a small pan and bring to the boil. Cover and simmer for 10 minutes. Remove from the heat and leave to stand, covered, for 1 hour. Mash, then sieve into a bowl. Reserve 3 tablespoons and use the remainder for another dish (see Cook's Tip).

Place the red pepper, onions, garlic, chilli and lemon grass in a liquidizer or food processor and blend. Heat the oil, add the pepper mixture and stir-fry for 5 minutes. Gradually blend in the tamarind paste, sugar, lime juice and salt to taste. Add the prawns and stir-fry for 5 minutes or until the prawns are just firm to the touch. Serve at once.

Cook's Tip

The tamarind paste can be stored in the refrigerator for use in other dishes for up to 2 weeks.

74 | *Pickled Haddock Steaks*

Preparation time
15 minutes, plus 12 hours chilling time

Cooking time
about 20 minutes

Serves 4

Calories
340 per portion

You will need
4 tablespoons oil
4 (225-g/8-oz) haddock steaks
2 onions, chopped
1 garlic clove, peeled
2.5 cm/1 inch piece root ginger, peeled
1 tablespoon coriander seeds
4 green chillies, seeded
5 tablespoons wine vinegar
½ teaspoon turmeric
4 curry leaves (see Cook's Tip)
salt

Heat the oil in a large frying pan, add the fish and fry on both sides until browned. Remove with a slotted spoon and set aside. Add the onions to the pan and fry until soft.

Put the garlic, ginger, coriander seeds, chillies and 1 tablespoon vinegar into a liquidizer or food processor and work to a paste. Add to the pan with the turmeric, curry leaves and salt to taste and fry for 3–4 minutes.

Add the remaining vinegar, bring to simmering point, stir well and add the fish. Cook, uncovered, for 3–4 minutes, until tender.

Place the fish in a dish, pour over all the juices and leave to cool. Cover and keep in the refrigerator for at least 12 hours. Serve cold.

Cook's Tip

Curry leaves, or kari patta, are the aromatic leaves of the sweet nim tree, available dried. They release an appetising smell when cooked.

75 | Curried Prawn Ring

Preparation time
25 minutes, plus
chilling time

Cooking time
about 25 minutes

Serves 4–6

Calories
360–240 per portion

You will need
350 g/12 oz long-grain rice
few saffron threads
1 tablespoon sunflower oil
1 tablespoon curry powder
8 spring onions, chopped
1 red pepper, seeded and
    chopped
50 g/2 oz pine nuts
75 g/3 oz sultanas
225 g/8 oz peeled prawns

For the dressing
4 tablespoons olive oil
2 tablespoons white wine vinegar
1 teaspoon dry mustard
1 teaspoon sugar
2 tablespoons chopped coriander
    leaves

Cook the rice in boiling salted water with the saffron added for 20 minutes until tender. Meanwhile, shake the dressing ingredients in a screw-topped jar to blend.

Drain the rice, place in a bowl and stir in the dressing while still warm. Cool slightly.

Heat the oil in a pan, add the curry powder, spring onions, red pepper, pine nuts and sultanas and cook, stirring for 1½ minutes. Add to the rice; leave to cool.

Stir in the prawns, then spoon the mixture into a lightly oiled 1.5-litre/2½-pint ring mould, pressing down well. Chill until required, then invert on to a serving plate to serve. Garnish as above if liked.

Cook's Tip

Other mixtures of shellfish or cooked fish can be used in this recipe instead of prawns – try using a mixture of cooked mussels, shrimps, clams, monkfish and scallops.

76 | Haddock in Chilli Sauce

Preparation time
5 minutes

Cooking time
15–20 minutes

Serves 4

Calories
350 per portion

You will need
4 tablespoons oil
2 large onions, sliced
3 cloves garlic, crushed
750 g/1½ lb haddock fillets, cut
    into chunks
2 tablespoons plain flour
1 teaspoon turmeric
4 green chillies, thinly sliced
2 tablespoons lemon juice
175 ml/6 fl oz thick coconut milk
    (see Cook's Tip recipe 3)
salt
chilli flowers to garnish (see
    Cook's Tip)

Heat the oil in a wok, add the onions and fry until soft and golden. Add the garlic and cook for 30 seconds. Remove from the pan with a slotted spoon and set aside.

Toss the fish in the flour, add to the pan and brown quickly on all sides. Drain on kitchen paper.

Return the onions and garlic to the wok, stir in the turmeric and chillies; cook for 1 minute. Stir in the lemon juice, coconut milk and salt to taste; simmer, uncovered, for 10 minutes, stirring until the sauce has thickened.

Return the fish to the wok and heat for 2–3 minutes. Spoon into a warmed serving dish and serve garnished with chilli flowers.

Cook's Tip

To make chilli flowers, shred the chilli lengthways, leaving 1 cm/½ inch attached at the stem end. Place in iced water for about 1 hour to open.

77 | Curried Crab

Preparation time
about 20 minutes

Cooking time
20 minutes

Serves 6

Calories
550 per portion

You will need
1 fresh coconut
75 g/3 oz ghee
1 large onion, sliced
4 garlic cloves, sliced
7.5 cm/3 inch piece root ginger,
  peeled and thinly sliced
2 teaspoons fenugreek seeds
2 teaspoons peppercorns
2 teaspoons chilli powder
2 teaspoons ground coriander
1 teaspoon turmeric
1 teaspoon salt
450 g/1 lb natural yogurt
300 ml/½ pint milk
450 g/1 lb crab meat

Prepare the coconut as in the Cook's Tip. Heat the ghee, add the onion, garlic and ginger and fry for 5 minutes. Add the fenugreek, peppercorns, chilli powder, coriander, turmeric and salt. Stir well and fry for 2–3 minutes, then add the coconut milk. Mix the yogurt with the milk and slowly stir into the pan. Bring to just below boiling point and simmer for 5–6 minutes.

Add the crab meat and sliced coconut and cook gently for 5 minutes. Serve at once.

78 | Poached Prawns with Piquant Dip Sauce

Preparation time
10 minutes

Cooking time
1–2 minutes

Serves 4

Calories
180 per portion

You will need
450 g/1 lb headless uncooked
  prawns
1 teaspoon salt
4–5 slices unpeeled root ginger

For the dip sauce
2 tablespoons oil
2–3 slices root ginger, shredded
2–3 spring onions, shredded
2–3 green and red chillies, seeded
  and finely shredded
3 tablespoons light soy sauce
1 tablespoon vinegar
1 tablespoon dry sherry or sake
pinch of sugar
1 teaspoon sesame oil

Wash the prawns; trim off the whiskers and legs but leave the tail pieces firmly attached

Bring 2 litres/3½ pints water to the boil in a large pan with the salt and sliced ginger. Add the prawns and poach for 1–2 minutes only; drain well.

To make the dip sauce, heat the oil in a small pan until very hot. Place the shredded ginger, spring onions and fresh chillies in a bowl. Slowly pour the hot oil over and mix in the remaining ingredients. Serve with the prawns.

Cook's Tip

Make holes in the eyes of the coconut, then drain out the liquid and reserve. Crack open the coconut and separate the flesh from the shell. Thinly slice ¼ of the coconut and blend the remainder in a liquidizer or food processor.

Add 600 ml/1 pint boiling water, stir for 5 minutes then strain through cheesecloth. Mix the strained liquid from the coconut with the prepared coconut milk. Use the coconut milk and sliced coconut as indicated above.

Cook's Tip

If slicing onions makes you cry, work under running water or, if you have time, chill the onions in the freezer for 10–15 minutes before peeling.

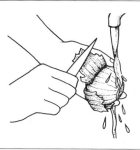

79 | Fillets of Sole with Mushrooms

Preparation time
20 minutes

Cooking time
5–10 minutes

Serves 3–4

Calories
300–220 per portion

You will need
450 g/1 lb sole fillets
1 egg white
1 tablespoon cornflour
oil for deep frying
225 g/8 oz button mushrooms,
    sliced
2–3 spring onions, shredded
1 slice root ginger, shredded
1 teaspoon sugar
1 teaspoon salt
1 tablespoon soy sauce
1 tablespoon sake or dry sherry
100 ml/4 fl oz fish stock
1 teaspoon sesame oil

Halve the fish fillets if they are large. Mix in a bowl with the egg white and cornflour. Heat the oil in a wok or deep frying pan and deep fry the fish until golden and crisp; drain on absorbent kitchen paper.

Pour off all but 2 tablespoons of the oil in the pan. Add the mushrooms, spring onions and ginger. Stir-fry for 30 seconds, then add the salt, sugar, soy sauce, sherry and stock. Bring to the boil, add the fish and simmer for 2 minutes. Sprinkle over the sesame oil and serve hot.

80 | Fish and Bean Curd Casserole

Preparation time
20 minutes

Cooking time
15–20 minutes

Serves 4

Calories
220 per portion

You will need
450 g/1 lb firm white fish fillets
1 tablespoon cornflour
2 tablespoons water
1 egg white
450 g/1 lb firm bean curd or tofu
a few Chinese or Cos lettuce
    leaves
3 tablespoons sake or dry sherry
2 tablespoons light soy sauce
1 teaspoon sugar
2 slices root ginger, peeled
3 spring onions, chopped
salt and pepper
300 ml/½ pint clear broth (see
    Cook's Tip recipe 10)
50 g/2 oz cooked ham, chopped
1 teaspoon sesame oil

Cut the fish into small pieces. Mix the cornflour to a paste with 2 tablespoons cold water, then mix with the egg white and use to coat the fish. Cut the bean curd into small cubes.

Line a flameproof casserole with the Chinese leaves or lettuce. Add the bean curd and fish pieces with the sherry, soy sauce, sugar, ginger, spring onions and salt and pepper to taste. Pour over the broth and sprinkle with the ham. Bring to the boil, cover, reduce the heat and simmer for 15–20 minutes.

Sprinkle with the sesame oil and serve at once.

Cook's Tip

This dish is not unlike the French Filets de Sole Bonne Femme. The fish can be skinned if liked, but leaving the skin on helps to keep the fish intact during cooking.

Cook's Tip

An easy way to separate an egg: break the egg over a saucer or shallow dish. Place an egg-cup (or small glass) over the yolk. Holding the egg-cup in place, tilt the saucer and pour off all the white into a small bowl.

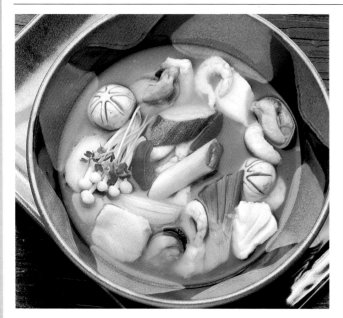

81 | *Spicy Fish with Vegetables*

Preparation time
20 minutes

Cooking time
10–15 minutes

Serves 4

Calories
170 per portion

You will need
600 ml/1 pint water
1 teaspoon chilli powder
1 tablespoon chilli sauce
1 teaspoon salt
450 g/1 lb cod fillets, cubed
20 shellfish (cooked mussels,
   prawns and scallops for
   example)
1 onion, cut into 8 pieces
20 button mushrooms, wiped
1 red pepper, cut into 8 pieces
1 garlic clove, crushed
4 spring onions, chopped
1 courgette, cut into 8 pieces
cress to garnish
enokitake mushrooms (optional)

Place the water, chilli powder, chilli sauce and salt in a pan and bring to the boil. Add the fish, shelled shellfish, onion, mushrooms, red pepper and garlic. Bring back to the boil then add the spring onions and courgette and simmer for 10 minutes or until just cooked.

Divide between 4 serving bowls and serve at once, sprinkled with the cress and enokitake mushrooms.

Cook's Tip

**This simple Korean fish stew
is quick to prepare. It is both
warming and filling and
makes a colourful winter dish.
Any combination of white fish
and shellfish may be used.**

82 | *Deep-Fried Prawn Balls*

Preparation time
30–40 minutes

Cooking time
about 3–5 minutes

Serves 4

Calories
320 per portion

You will need
450 g/1 lb peeled prawns
50 g/2 oz pork fat
1 egg white
2 tablespoons cornflour
1 tablespoon brandy or rum
1 teaspoon finely chopped root
   ginger
salt and pepper
oil for deep frying

Finely chop the prawns with the pork fat. Place in a bowl with the egg white, cornflour, brandy or rum, ginger and salt and pepper to taste. Stir well and leave to stand for 30 minutes.

Divide and form the mixture into about 24 small balls. Heat the oil and deep-fry the balls, in batches, until golden. Drain on absorbent kitchen towels.

Just before serving reheat the oil and re-fry the fish balls for a few seconds. Drain and place in a serving bowl. Garnish as shown in the photograph if liked.

Cook's Tip

**Cook these balls up to 3 hours
in advance, then deep-fry or
crisp in a moderate oven just
before serving.**

83 | *Squid with Herbs*

Preparation time
about 10 minutes

Cooking time
2 minutes

Serves 4

Calories
230 per portion

You will need
1 kg/2 lb prepared baby squid (see Cook's Tip)
salt
pepper
4 tablespoons olive oil
3–4 cloves garlic, thickly sliced
2 tablespoons chopped thyme
1 tablespoon chopped parsley
juice of ½ lemon

For the garnish
lemon slices
tiny bunches of thyme

Cut the squid into slices; cut the tentacles in half if they are large. Season with salt and pepper to taste.

Heat the oil in a wok, add the garlic and cook gently until browned, then discard the garlic by removing with a slotted spoon. Increase the heat, add the squid and cook briskly for just under 1 minute. Sprinkle with the herbs and lemon juice. Serve immediately, garnished with lemon and tiny bunches of thyme.

84 | *Stir-Fried Squid with Vegetables*

Preparation time
30 minutes

Cooking time
about 10 minutes

Serves 4

Calories
270 per portion

You will need
400 g/14 oz squid, cleaned
2 slices root ginger, chopped
1 tablespoon sake or dry sherry
1 tablespoon cornflour
15 g/½ oz dried wood ears, soaked for 20 minutes
4 tablespoons vegetable oil
2 spring onions, chopped
225 g/8 oz cauliflower or broccoli florets
2 carrots, cut into diamond shaped chunks
1 teaspoon salt
1 teaspoon sugar
1 teaspoon sesame oil

Cut the prepared squid into rings and thin slices. Place in a bowl with half the ginger, the sake or sherry and corn-flour. Mix well and leave to stand for 20 minutes. Meanwhile, drain the wood ears and break into small pieces, discarding the hard bits.

Heat 2 tablespoons of the oil in a wok or frying pan, add the spring onions and remaining ginger, then the cauliflower or broccoli, carrots and wood ears. Stir, then add the salt and sugar and continue cooking until the vegetables are tender, adding a little water if necessary. Remove from the pan with a slotted spoon and drain.

Heat the remaining oil in the pan, add the squid and stir-fry for about 1 minute. Return the vegetables to the pan, add the sesame oil and mix well. Serve hot.

Cook's Tip

To prepare squid, draw back the rim of the body pouch to locate the quill-shaped pen and pull free to discard. Separate the body from the tentacles by pulling gently apart just below the eyes – the inedible head and ink-sack will come away together. Slip a finger under the skin and peel it away gently.

Cook's Tip

The squid's ink sacs contain a dark brown liquid, which can be used as a basis for a sauce in which to cook it.

85 | Carp with Sweet and Sour Sauce

Preparation time
40 minutes, including
soaking time

Cooking time
about 15 minutes

Serves 4

Calories
350 per portion

You will need
15 g/½ oz dried wood ears,
    soaked for 20 minutes
1½–2 lb/750 g–1 kg carp, cleaned
2 teaspoons salt
3 tablespoons flour
4 tablespoons vegetable oil
2–3 spring onions, shredded
2 slices root ginger, shredded
1 garlic clove, chopped
15 g/½ oz bamboo shoots, sliced
50 g/2 oz waterchestnuts, sliced
1 red pepper, shredded
3 tablespoons wine vinegar
3 tablespoons sugar
2 tablespoons soy sauce
2 tablespoons sake or sherry
2 teaspoons cornflour
150 ml/¼ pint stock or water

Drain the wood ears and slice thinly, discarding the hard bits. Remove the tail and fins of the fish but leave the head on. Make diagonal slashes along both sides, dry well then rub with 1 teaspoon salt and coat all over with flour. Heat the oil until very hot, lower the heat, add the fish and fry for 4–5 minutes on each side until golden and crisp. Drain and keep hot.

Add the spring onions, ginger, garlic, the wood ears, bamboo shoots, waterchestnuts, red pepper and remaining salt and vinegar. Mix the remaining ingredients together, stir into the pan and cook until thick. Pour over the fish to serve.

Cook's Tip

Carp is a symbol of good fortune in China, so it is served at New Year and other festivities. Snapper can be used instead, if liked.

86 | Sashimi

Preparation time
20 minutes

Serves 4

Calories
200 per portion

You will need
675 g/1½ lb bream, tuna or other
    salt water fish, filleted
350 g/12 oz daikon or white
    radish, shredded
1 carrot, shredded
4–5 spring onions, shredded
few mangetout
few cooked, unshelled prawns
1 tablespoon wasabi (see Cook's
    Tip)
few lemon wedges
1 tablespoon freshly grated ginger
shoyu to taste (see Cook's Tip)

Remove any skin, blood and dark sections from the fish and cut diagonally into slices about 2.5 cm/1 inch long and 5 mm/¼ inch thick.

Arrange the shredded radish, carrot and spring onion in mounds on a serving plate with the mangetout, fish slices and prawns.

Mix the wasabi to a thick paste with a little water. Place on the plate with the lemon wedges and ginger.

To serve, pour shoyu into individual bowls, then allow each diner to add wasabi and ginger to their own bowl of shoyu according to taste. The fish and vegetables are then dipped into the sauce before eating. Serve with Japanese-style medium-grain rice.

Cook's Tip

Wasabi is green horseradish available both fresh and dried. Shoyu is a light soy sauce made in Japan – do not substitute Chinese soy sauce or other soy sauces, their flavour is completely different and will spoil the dish.

87 | Prawn Cutlets

Preparation time
10 minutes

Cooking time
2–3 minutes

Serves 2

Calories
230 per portion

You will need
8 Dublin Bay or large king prawns
   in their shells
1 tablespoon dry sherry
1 egg, beaten
2 tablespoons cornflour
oil for deep frying
fresh coriander leaves to garnish

Clean, de-vein and split the prawns to make cutlets (see Cook's Tip). Sprinkle with the sherry, dip in the egg and coat in the cornflour. Repeat the coating once more.

Heat the oil to 180 C/350 F and deep-fry the prawns for 2–3 minutes. Drain on absorbent kitchen paper and serve at once garnished with fresh coriander. Serve plain or with soy sauce.

88 | Steamed Whole Fish

Preparation time
about 45 minutes

Cooking time
12 minutes

Serves 4

Calories
380 per portion

You will need
3 slices root ginger, chopped
2 teaspoons salt
1.25 kg/2½ lb small fish (trout,
   sole or mackerel for example)
3 tablespoons soy sauce
1½ teaspoons sugar
1 tablespoon wine vinegar
2 tablespoons oil
2–3 rashers bacon, shredded
3–4 large dried Chinese
   mushrooms, soaked for 20
   minutes, drained, stemmed and
   shredded
4 spring onions, chopped

Mix the ginger and salt and rub over the fish inside and out; leave for 30 minutes.

Mix the soy sauce with the sugar, vinegar and oil, pour over the fish and leave for 15 minutes.

Place the fish on a heatproof dish and spoon over the marinade. Sprinkle with the bacon, mushrooms and spring onions. Place on a rack in a wok or large pan containing water. Cover and steam vigorously for 12 minutes. The fish is cooked when it will flake easily using chopsticks. Serve hot.

Cook's Tip

To make prawn cutlets, hold the prawns firmly by the tail and remove the shell, leaving the tail shell intact. Cut the prawns in half lengthways almost through to the tail and remove the dark intestinal vein. Then flatten the prawns.

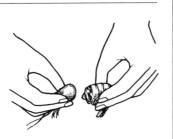

Cook's Tip

This Chinese quick-steaming method of cooking fish is ideal for fresh whole fish or fillets of larger fish such as salmon, sea bream or striped bass.

89 | Braised Prawns

Preparation time
5 minutes plus 1–2
hours marinating time

Cooking time
about 5 minutes

Serves 4

Calories
180 per portion

You will need
1 teaspoon salt
1 egg white
2 tablespoons cornflour
225 g/8 oz raw peeled prawns
225 g/8 oz lard
2 tablespoons dry sherry
4 tablespoons stock
1 tablespoon water
1 teaspoon sesame oil

Mix the salt with the egg white and 1 tablespoon of the cornflour. Add the prawns and leave to marinate in the refrigerator for 1–2 hours.

Heat the lard in a pan. Add the prawns and stir to separate them, then lift out with a slotted spoon. Pour off the excess lard, leaving a small amount in the pan. Add the sherry, stock and prawns and bring to the boil. Dissolve the remaining cornflour in the water and add to the pan, stir until thickened. Add the sesame oil and serve.

90 | Soy-Braised Cod or Halibut Steaks

Preparation time
15 minutes

Cooking time
about 12 minutes

Serves 4

Calories
260 per portion

You will need
50 g/2 oz lard
3–4 spring onions, chopped
2–3 slices root ginger, chopped
450 g/1 lb cod or halibut steaks,
    quartered
2 tablespoons sherry
2 tablespoons soy sauce
1 tablespoon sugar
100 ml/4 fl oz water
1 tablespoon cornflour dissolved in
    1½ tablespoons water
1 teaspoon sesame oil
shredded spring onion to garnish

Melt the lard in a pan over a high heat. Add the spring onions and ginger and stir-fry for a few seconds. Add the fish pieces and stir very gently to separate. Add the sherry and bring to the boil, then stir in the soy sauce, sugar and water. Simmer for about 10 minutes.

Add the cornflour mixture and simmer until thickened. Add the sesame oil and serve hot, garnished with shredded spring onion.

Cook's Tip

Braised Prawns can be served either hot or cold. Serve on a bed of shredded lettuce.

Cook's Tip

Any other firm white fish may be used for this recipe, such as haddock, whiting or plaice. Use fish steaks or fillets, depending upon the fish type.

91 | *Crispy Skin Fish*

Preparation time
10 minutes, plus 3½
hours standing time

Cooking time
about 10 minutes

Serves 4

Calories
270 per portion

You will need
675 g/1½ lb small fish
3–4 slices root ginger, chopped
1 tablespoon salt
1½ tablespoons plain flour
oil for deep frying

Slit the fish along the belly, clean and rinse thoroughly but leave the heads and tails intact. Rub the fish inside and out with the ginger and salt. Leave for 3 hours. Rub with the flour and leave for a further 30 minutes.

Heat the oil to 180C/350F and deep-fry the fish in batches for 3–4 minutes, or until crisp and golden. Drain on absorbent kitchen paper and serve hot.

92 | *Dry Fried Herring*

Preparation time
about 20 minutes

Cooking time
30 minutes

Serves 4

Calories
260 per portion

You will need
about 1 teaspoon chilli powder
1½ teaspoons turmeric
1 teaspoon ground ginger
1 teaspoon garlic powder or paste
salt and pepper
450 g/1 lb herring fillets, cut into
    5-cm/2-inch pieces
oil for frying
1 lemon, sliced to garnish

Mix together the chilli powder, turmeric, ginger, garlic and salt and pepper to taste. Rub this mixture into the fish and set aside to marinate for 10–15 minutes.

Heat a little oil and fry the fish in two batches until golden brown. Remove and drain the fish. Serve hot, garnished with lemon slices.

Cook's Tip

This recipe is suitable for small fish such as whiting, herring and small trout. Make sure the fish are fried until really crisp for success.

Cook's Tip

The herring is a bony, delicately flavoured fish and because of this it is generally fried rather than made into a curry. Cut the herring into pieces with or without the roe as liked.

93 | *Baked Spiced Fish*

Preparation time
10 minutes plus
overnight marinating

Cooking time
30 minutes

Oven temperature
180 C, 350 F, gas 4

Serves 4

Calories
180 per portion with
white fish (400 per
portion with oily fish)

You will need
250 ml/8 fl oz natural yogurt
1 onion, chopped
1 garlic clove, chopped
1 teaspoon grated root ginger
1 tablespoon vinegar
1½ teaspoons ground cumin
pinch of chilli powder
1 kg/2 lb whole fish or 675 g/
    1½ lb fish fillets (see Cook's
    Tip)
juice of 1 lemon
1 teaspoon salt

For the garnish
lemon slices
fresh coriander leaves

Put a quarter of the yogurt, the onion, garlic, ginger, vinegar, cumin and chilli powder in a liquidizer or food processor and blend to a smooth sauce. Add the remaining yogurt.

Score the fish and place in an ovenproof dish. Rub with lemon juice and sprinkle with the salt. Pour over the yogurt marinade, cover and leave to marinate overnight.

Cover the fish with foil and bake for 30 minutes. Serve hot, garnished with lemon slices and coriander leaves.

94 | *Crab Omelette*

Preparation time
10 minutes

Cooking time
about 1–2 minutes

Serves 3–4

Calories
360–270 per portion

You will need
2 spring onions
4 eggs, beaten
salt
3 tablespoons oil
2 slices root ginger, shredded
175 g/6 oz crab meat
1 tablespoon sake or dry sherry
1 tablespoon soy sauce
2 teaspoons sugar

For the garnish (optional)
½ lettuce, shredded
tomato water-lily (see Cook's Tip)
seedless grape

Cut the white part of the spring onions into 2.5-cm/1-inch lengths. Chop the green part finely and beat into the eggs with salt to taste.

Heat the oil and add the white spring onions and the ginger, then the crab and sake or sherry. Stir-fry for a few seconds, then add the soy sauce and sugar.

Lower the heat, pour in the egg mixture and cook for a further 30 seconds. Transfer to a warmed serving plate, garnish with shredded lettuce and a tomato water-lily with a grape on top. Serve at once.

Cook's Tip

When selecting the fish for this dish you will find that whole fish give the best results – try bream, snapper or flounder for example. You can use an oily fish such as mackerel but increase the amount of vinegar to 2 tablespoons. If using fillets, select cod or a similar chunky fish, or use fish steaks.

Cook's Tip

To make a tomato water-lily, make zig-zag cuts around the middle of a tomato using a small, sharp knife. Make sure the cuts go right through to the centre. Separate the two halves carefully.

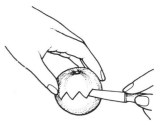

95 | Steamed Sweet and Sour Fish

Preparation time
10 minutes

Cooking time
12–15 minutes

Serves 4

Calories
150 per portion

You will need
1 large whole plaice, cleaned
salt
2 (2.5-cm/1-inch) pieces root
   ginger, shredded
3 spring onions, sliced

For the sauce
150 ml/¼ pint fish or chicken
   stock
1 tablespoon soy sauce
1 tablespoon sugar
1 tablespoon wine vinegar
1 tablespoon dry sherry
1 tablespoon tomato purée
1 teaspoon chilli sauce
pinch of salt
1 tablespoon cornflour

Score the fish by making 3 diagonal cuts on each side. Rub the fish with salt and sprinkle with the ginger and spring onions. Put on an ovenproof plate and place in a steamer. Steam for 12–15 minutes until tender.

Meanwhile, make the sauce. Mix all the ingredients except the cornflour, together in a small pan. Bring to the boil and cook for 1 minute. Blend the cornflour with 2 tablespoons water and stir into the sauce. Cook, stirring until thickened.

Carefully lift the plaice on to a serving dish and spoon over the sauce. Serve hot.

Cook's Tip

Fresh or frozen plaice can be used for this recipe. Garnish with fresh coriander leaves and tomato flowers if liked.

96 | Braised Fish with Black Bean Sauce

Preparation time
20 minutes

Cooking time
10–15 minutes

Serves 4

Calories
260 per portion

You will need
3 tablespoons black beans (see
   Cook's Tip)
2 tablespoons oil
2 spring onions, chopped
2.5 cm/1 inch piece root ginger,
   chopped
1 small red pepper, cored, seeded
   and chopped
2 celery sticks, chopped
2 tablespoons soy sauce
2 tablespoons dry sherry
4 cod or haddock cutlets, each
   weighing 150 g/5 oz
shredded spring onion to garnish

Soak the black beans in warm water for 10 minutes; drain.

Heat the oil in a wok or deep frying pan, add the spring onions, ginger, red pepper and celery and stir-fry for 1 minute. Stir in the soy sauce and sherry. Place the fish on top of the vegetables and simmer for 5–10 minutes until almost tender, depending upon the thickness of the fish. Spoon over the black beans and cook for 2 minutes.

Arrange the fish on a warmed serving dish and spoon the sauce over. Serve hot, garnished with shredded spring onion.

Cook's Tip

Black beans are salted, fermented beans with a strong, salty flavour. They are sold in packs or by weight in Chinese supermarkets. They must be soaked for 5–10 minutes before use.

97 | *Spiced Prawns in Coconut*

Preparation time
5 minutes

Cooking time
15 minutes

Serves 4

Calories
280 per portion

You will need
4 tablespoons oil
1 large onion, sliced
4 garlic cloves, sliced
2 teaspoons ground coriander
1 teaspoon turmeric
1 teaspoon chilli powder
½ teaspoon ground ginger
½ teaspoon salt
pepper to taste
2 tablespoons vinegar
200 ml/½ pint coconut milk (see Cook's Tip)
2 tablespoons tomato purée
450 g/1 lb peeled prawns

Heat the oil in a wok or deep frying pan, add the onion and garlic and fry gently until soft and golden.

Mix the spices together in a bowl, add the salt and pepper, stir in the vinegar and mix to a paste. Add to the wok and fry for 3 minutes, stirring constantly.

Stir in the coconut milk and tomato purée and simmer for 5 minutes. Stir in the prawns and heat through for 2–3 minutes, until well coated with sauce. Serve at once garnished as shown if liked.

Cook's Tip

Coconut milk can be bought in a very convenient form as coconut granules. Simply make up a thin or thick coconut milk following the packet instructions.

98 | *Hot Jumbo Prawns*

Preparation time
10 minutes

Cooking time
6 minutes

Serves 4

Calories
370 per portion

You will need
1 teaspoon very finely chopped root ginger
3 spring onions, chopped
12 giant Pacific prawns, shelled
3 tablespoons self-raising flour
pinch of salt
½–1 teaspoon chilli powder
½ teaspoon paprika
3 teaspoons dry sherry
1 egg, beaten
1 tablespoon chopped fresh coriander
oil for deep frying
tomato roses and coriander leaves to garnish

Mix together the ginger, spring onions and prawns. Place the flour, salt, chilli powder to taste and paprika in a bowl. Add the sherry and egg and beat to a smooth batter. Fold in the coriander and prawn mixture.

Heat the oil to 160 C/325 F and deep fry half the battered prawns for 2–3 minutes, until golden. Drain on absorbent kitchen paper and keep hot while frying the remainder.

Arrange on a warmed serving dish and garnish with coriander leaves and tomato roses. Serve at once.

Cook's Tip

To make a tomato rose, thinly pare all the skin from a tomato, taking care to keep it in one piece. Tightly curl the skin into a circle and use at once.

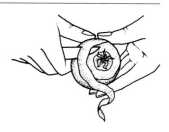

99 | *Crab in Black Bean Sauce*

Preparation time
6 minutes

Cooking time
12 minutes

Serves 4

Calories
260 per portion

You will need
2 tablespoons oil
2 tablespoons salted black beans,
   coarsely chopped
2 garlic cloves, crushed
2 tablespoons chopped root
   ginger
4 spring onions, chopped
225 g/8 oz lean minced pork
1 large cooked crab, cut into
   pieces
2 tablespoons dry sherry
300 ml/½ pint chicken stock
2 eggs, beaten
1–2 teaspoons sesame oil
spring onion flowers to garnish

Heat the oil in a wok or deep frying pan, add the black beans, garlic, ginger and spring onions and fry briskly for 30 seconds. Add the pork and brown quickly for 1 minute. Add the crab, sherry and stock and boil rapidly for 8-10 minutes.

Combine the eggs and sesame oil and stir into the wok. Stir for 30 seconds, until the egg has cooked in strands. Transfer to a warmed serving dish and garnish with spring onion flowers. Serve at once.

100 | *Prawns with Almonds*

Preparation time
4 minutes

Cooking time
7 minutes

Serves 4

Calories
300 per portion

You will need
75 g/3 oz blanched almonds
350 g/12 oz peeled prawns
2 teaspoons cornflour
1 heaped teaspoon finely chopped
   root ginger
1 small garlic clove, crushed
2 tablespoons oil
1 celery stick, finely chopped
2 teaspoons soy sauce
2 teaspoons sherry
2 tablespoons water
pepper
spring onion flowers to garnish

Brush a frying pan with oil, add the almonds, then heat and toss until golden. Drain well.

Place the prawns in a bowl with the cornflour, ginger and garlic and mix well.

Heat the oil in the pan, add the prawn mixture and celery and stir-fry for 2–3 minutes. Add the soy sauce, sherry, water and pepper to taste. Bring to the boil, add the almonds and heat for 30 seconds. Serve hot, garnished with spring onion flowers.

Cook's Tip

Crab in Black Bean Sauce comes from southern China, where minced pork is often added to a fish dish to extend the dish. The salted black beans give a traditional flavour. The crab is cooked in the shell to protect the meat **during cooking – the easiest way of eating it is with the fingers!**

Cook's Tip

Prawns with Almonds has the traditional delicacy of Chinese food. It is flavoured with fresh root ginger – a knobbly root with a sandy coloured skin. Cut off the knobs and peel just as you would a small potato.

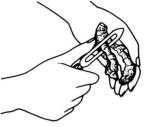

101 | Prawns with Asparagus

Preparation time
20 minutes, including marinating time

Cooking time
4 minutes

Serves 4

Calories
200 per portion

You will need
175 g/6 oz fresh asparagus, cut into 2.5-cm/1-inch pieces
½ teaspoon salt
4 tablespoons dry sherry
1 teaspoon light soy sauce
450 g/1 lb peeled prawns
2 tablespoons oil
2 garlic cloves, thinly sliced
2 teaspoons chopped root ginger
4 spring onions, chopped

Blanch the asparagus in boiling salted water for 2 minutes; drain well and set aside.

Mix the sherry with the soy sauce. Stir in the prawns and leave to marinate for 15 minutes.

Heat the oil in a wok or deep frying pan and quickly stir-fry the garlic, ginger and half the spring onions. Add the prawns and marinade, and the asparagus and stir-fry for 1–2 minutes, until the ingredients are hot. Sprinkle with the remaining spring onions and serve at once.

102 | Vinegar Fish

Preparation time
10 minutes

Cooking time
12–15 minutes

Serves 4

Calories
260 per portion

You will need
1 teaspoon turmeric
1 teaspoon salt
450 g/1 lb haddock or cod steaks
3 tablespoons oil
2 onions, sliced
2–3 green chillies, thinly sliced
2 garlic cloves
2.5 cm/1 inch piece root ginger, cut into strips
2 tablespoons white wine vinegar
4 tablespoons water
fresh coriander leaves to garnish

Mix the turmeric and salt together on a plate. Coat the fish in the mixture. Heat the oil in a frying pan, add the fish and fry gently on both sides for 1–2 minutes. Lift out the fish and set aside.

Add the onions, chillies, garlic and ginger to the pan and fry, stirring, until golden. Stir in the vinegar and water. Put in the fish, cover and cook gently for 5–6 minutes or until cooked through.

Transfer to a warmed serving dish and garnish with the coriander to serve.

Cook's Tip

Seafood is especially important in Chinese cuisine. Much of the fish being sold live and taken home for cooking. As seafood is so delicate it requires minimum handling and simple cooking. The most common methods include steaming, deep-frying, braising and, as shown here, stir-frying. Serve this dish with a simple boiled or fried rice accompaniment.

Cook's Tip

This is a recipe from the west coast of India. Here sourness is introduced to the fish with vinegar instead of the usual way with tamarind. Serve with lentils, chapati and a bowl of natural yogurt.

103 | Chinese Steamed Trout

Preparation time
10 minutes

Cooking time
15 minutes

Serves 4

Calories
350 per portion

You will need
1 tablespoon sesame oil
1 tablespoon light soy sauce
1 tablespoon dry sherry
2 rainbow trout, about 1 kg/2 lb
   total weight, cleaned
4 garlic cloves, sliced
6 spring onions, shredded
5 cm/2 inch piece root ginger,
   shredded
2 tablespoons dry white vermouth
2 tablespoons oil

Mix together the sesame oil, soy sauce and sherry and use to brush the inside and skin of the fish. Mix together the garlic, spring onions and ginger and place a quarter of the mixture inside each fish.

Place the fish on a heatproof plate, scatter over the remaining garlic mixture and pour over the vermouth and oil. Put the plate in a wok or steamer and steam vigorously for 15 minutes, or until the fish are tender.

Arrange on a warmed serving dish, pour over the juices and serve at once.

104 | Coconut Fish

Preparation time
10 minutes

Cooking time
15 minutes

Serves 4

Calories
450 per portion

You will need
2 tablespoons oil
4 green chillies, seeded and
   chopped
2 garlic cloves, chopped
2.5 cm/1 inch piece root ginger,
   finely chopped
100 g/4 oz creamed coconut
1 kg/2 lb thick haddock fillets,
   skinned and cubed
salt
juice of 2 lemons

Heat the oil in a large frying pan, add the chillies, garlic and ginger and fry for 3 minutes. Add the creamed coconut and, when bubbling, add the fish and salt to taste. Stir well.

Cook for 3–4 minutes, stirring and breaking up the fish as it cooks. As soon as all the fish is cooked through, pour in the lemon juice, stir well and serve.

Cook's Tip

If you do not have a Chinese steamer, place the food on a heatproof plate which fits into a wok with a lid. Place a strip of foil under the plate to enable it to be lifted in and out of the wok with ease.

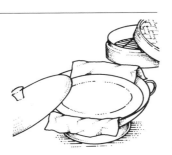

Cook's Tip

Coconut is much used in food in southern India. It is particularly good with fish in this dish which is simple to make and not too chilli hot. Serve it with boiled rice and moong dhal.

105 | Sole with Saté Sauce

Preparation time
35 minutes

Cooking time
20 minutes

Serves 4

Calories
750 per portion

You will need
1 teaspoon each of coriander, cumin and fennel seeds, crushed
2 garlic cloves, crushed
100 g/4 oz crunchy peanut butter
1 teaspoon dark soft brown sugar
2 green chillies, seeded and chopped
150 g/5 oz creamed coconut
3 tablespoons lemon juice
25 g/1 oz butter
1 shallot, finely chopped
1 tablespoon each of chopped chives, tarragon and parsley
grated rind of ½ lemon
8 Dover or lemon sole fillets
1 egg, beaten
4–5 tablespoons fresh breadcrumbs

To make the sauce, heat a wok or frying pan, add the crushed seeds and stir-fry for 2 minutes. Add the garlic, peanut butter, sugar, chillies and creamed coconut dissolved in 450 ml/¾ pint water, stir well and cook gently for 7–8 minutes. Stir in the lemon juice and keep warm.

Melt the butter in a pan, add the shallot and cook for 1 minute. Stir in the herbs and lemon rind. Cool slightly, then divide between the fish. Roll up each fillet, secure with wooden cocktail sticks, dip in egg, then coat in breadcrumbs. Deep fry for 4–5 minutes until golden. Drain and serve with the sauce.

Cook's Tip

This fish dish is particularly enhanced by the addition of fresh herbs, which bring out its delicate flavour. The secret of using fresh herbs is that they should be gathered and cooked immediately, so that the flavour is captured in the food and not lost during storage.

106 | Pineapple Prawn Curry

Preparation time
15 minutes

Cooking time
15 minutes

Serves 4

Calories
450 per portion

You will need
2 garlic cloves
1 small onion, quartered
2 green chillies, chopped
50 g/2 oz butter
1 bunch spring onions, chopped
450 g/1 lb raw peeled prawns
1 large green pepper, cored, seeded and coarsely chopped
150 ml/¼ pint double cream
salt
1 small pineapple, cut into chunks

Put the garlic, onion and green chillies in a liquidizer or food processor and work to a paste.

Melt the butter in a large frying pan, add the spring onions, prawns and green pepper and cook, stirring constantly until the prawns turn pink. Add the prepared paste and fry, stirring, for 2 minutes.

Add the cream, a spoonful at a time, and when it has all been incorporated, season with salt to taste. Stir in the pineapple. Cover and simmer for 5 minutes, then serve at once.

Cook's Tip

This pale creamy prawn curry should be cooked at the last possible moment for freshness. The pineapple helps to give the curry a little bite or acidity. Use fresh pineapple – canned is too sweet and bland.

107 | *Spicy Prawns*

Preparation time
8 minutes

Cooking time
15–20 minutes

Serves 4–6

Calories
280–190 per portion

You will need
450 g/1 lb peeled prawns
1 teaspoon ground coriander
1 heaped tablespoon chopped
	parsley
1 egg, beaten
40 g/1½ oz fresh wholewheat
	breadcrumbs
3 tablespoons oil
2 onions, finely chopped
1 garlic clove, crushed
¼ teaspoon chilli powder
½ teaspoon ground ginger
¼ teaspoon ground bay leaves
150 ml/¼ pint hot water
juice of 1 lemon

Mince the prawns and mix with the coriander and parsley. Divide and shape into walnut-sized balls; dip into the egg and coat in the breadcrumbs. Set aside.

Heat 2 tablespoons of the oil in a frying pan, add the prawn balls and fry until golden. Remove and keep warm. Heat the remaining oil, add the onions and fry until brown. Stir in the garlic, chilli, ginger and ground bay leaves and cook, stirring, for about 5 minutes.

Add the hot water, bring to the boil, then simmer for 8–10 minutes. Stir in the lemon juice. Serve the sauce with the prawn balls.

108 | *Prawns in Chilli Sauce*

Preparation time
6 minutes

Cooking time
6 minutes

Serves 4

Calories
140 per portion

You will need
1 tablespoon oil
3 spring onions, chopped
2 teaspoons chopped root ginger
225 g/8 oz peeled prawns
100 g/4 oz mangetout
½ teaspoon chilli powder
1 teaspoon tomato purée
¼ teaspoon salt
½ teaspoon sugar
1 tablespoon dry sherry
½ teaspoon sesame oil
whole prawns in shell to garnish

Heat the oil in a wok or deep frying pan, add the spring onions and ginger and stir-fry for 30 seconds. Add the prawns, mangetout, chilli powder, tomato purée, salt, sugar and sherry and stir-fry briskly for 5 minutes. Sprinkle over the sesame oil and serve at once, garnished with whole prawns.

Cook's Tip

Spicy Prawns has the pungent, hot flavour of Indian food. Serve with rice and a green salad for a main meal.

Cook's Tip

Prawns in Chilli Sauce originates from the western Szechuan region of China, where the emphasis is on hotness of food combined with pungent flavoured vegetables. Serve with plain rice or noodles.

109 | *Tandoori Sole*

Preparation time
10 minutes, plus 1 hour
marinating time

Cooking time
15 minutes

Oven temperature
180 C, 350 F, gas 4

Serves 2

Calories
300 per portion

You will need
½ teaspoon chilli powder
½ teaspoon turmeric
½ teaspoon ground coriander
½ teaspoon ground cumin
1 teaspoon ground ginger
½ teaspoon garam masala (see
  Cook's Tip recipe 67)
salt and pepper
275 g/10 oz natural yogurt
2 garlic cloves, crushed
2 drops red food colouring
2 lemon sole, skinned and filleted
  (see Cook's Tip)

Mix all the spices together, adding salt and pepper to taste. Add to the yogurt with the garlic and food colouring and stir well. Mix with the fish and leave to marinate for 1 hour.

Pour boiling water into a roasting pan to come halfway up the sides. Put a grill rack in the pan and place the marinated fish on the rack. Pour any remaining marinade over the fish. Cook for 15 minutes. Garnish as shown if liked. Serve at once.

110 | *Sweet and Sour Fish*

Preparation time
5 minutes

Cooking time
7 minutes

Serves 4

Calories
180 per portion

You will need
¼ teaspoon ground ginger
2 teaspoons cornflour
450 g/1 lb haddock or cod fillets,
  cut into small pieces
1 tablespoon oil

For the sauce
1 (227-g/8-oz) can tomatoes,
  drained and chopped
1 tablespoon soy sauce
1 tablespoon tomato purée
2 teaspoons cornflour
5 tablespoons water
2 tablespoons sherry
1 teaspoon brown sugar
chopped parsley to garnish

Mix the ginger with the cornflour and sprinkle over the fish. Heat the oil in a frying pan, add the fish and fry for 2–3 minutes, stirring. Remove from the pan with a slotted spoon and keep warm.

Wipe the pan clean with kitchen paper and lower the heat. Add the tomatoes and soy sauce. Mix the remaining ingredients together, then pour into the pan and cook, stirring until thickened. Add the fish and heat through for a few seconds. Sprinkle with parsley and serve at once.

Cook's Tip

To skin fish, place the fish skin down on a board, rub your fingers with salt and hold the tail end. With a sharp knife, cut between the skin and flesh at an acute angle, working from the tail end.

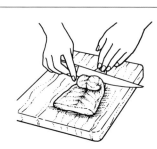

Cook's Tip

This speedy dish makes a good main meal for those in a hurry. Serve it with boiled rice and stir-fried mixed vegetables if liked.

111 | Stir-Fried Fish with Vegetables

Preparation time
5 minutes, plus 15 minutes standing time

Cooking time
4 minutes

Serves 4

Calories
220 per portion

You will need
450 g/1 lb cod fillet, skinned and cut into wide strips
1 teaspoon salt
1 tablespoon oil
2 rashers back bacon, shredded
50 g/2 oz cooked peas
50 g/2 oz cooked sweetcorn
6 tablespoons chicken stock or water
2 teaspoons dry sherry
2 teaspoons soy sauce
1 teaspoon sugar
1 teaspoon cornflour
1 teaspoon water

Sprinkle the fish fillets with the salt and leave to stand for 15 minutes.

Heat the oil in a frying pan, add the fish and bacon and stir-fry for 3 minutes. Add the remaining ingredients, except the cornflour and water, and bring to the boil. Blend the cornflour with the water and stir in. Cook for 1 minute.

Serve at once, garnished as shown if liked.

Cook's Tip

In Chinese cooking fish is often stir-fried with vegetables that retain their colour and nutritional value. Fresh, dried and pickled vegetables are used, as are numerous soy bean-based products from bean curd to soy sauce flavourings. The recipe above combines fish with peas, sweetcorn and soy sauce.

112 | Steamed Mussels

Preparation time
40 minutes

Cooking time
10–15 minutes

Serves 6

Calories
250 per portion

You will need
1 kg/2¼ lb mussels
100 g/4 oz ghee
1 large onion, chopped
2 garlic cloves, chopped
2 teaspoons desiccated coconut
2 teaspoons salt
1 teaspoon turmeric
1 teaspoon chilli powder
1 teaspoon black pepper
150 ml/¼ pint vinegar
450 g/1 lb natural yogurt
2 teaspoons garam masala
juice of 2 lemons

Prepare the fish as in the Cook's Tip. Heat the ghee, add the onion and garlic and fry for 5 minutes. Add the coconut and salt and fry until browned. Add the turmeric, chilli powder and pepper and fry for 1 minute. Add the vinegar and shellfish, cover and bring to the boil; cook for about 5 minutes or until the shells open, then remove from the heat.

Remove the empty half shells and discard. Arrange the remainder in a serving dish. Pour the cooking liquid into a liquidizer or food processor with the yogurt and garam masala and blend for 1 minute. Reheat until hot but not boiling. Pour over the shellfish, sprinkle with lemon juice and serve at once.

Cook's Tip

Scrub the mussels under cold running water and pull away the black hairs known as the 'beard' with a sharp tug. Leave to soak for 30 minutes. Discard any mussels that are not tightly shut or that do not shut quickly when tapped.

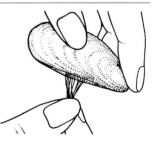

117 | Stuffed Peppers

Preparation time
20 minutes

Cooking time
about 40 minutes

Serves 4

Calories
470 per portion

You will need
5 tablespoons oil
1 onion, finely chopped
2 teaspoons ground coriander
1 teaspoon ground cumin
½ teaspoon chilli powder
350 g/12 oz minced beef
3 tablespoons long-grain rice
salt
4 large green or red peppers,
  sliced lengthways, cored and
  seeded
1 (400-g/14-oz) can tomatoes

Heat 3 tablespoons of the oil in a pan. Add the onion and fry until golden. Add the spices and cook for 2 minutes. Add the minced beef and fry, stirring, until browned. Add the rice and salt to taste and cook for 2 minutes. Leave to cool, then fill the pepper shells with the mixture.

Heat the remaining oil in a pan just large enough to hold the peppers. Add the peppers, pour a little of the tomato juice into each pepper and the remaining juice and tomatoes into the pan, seasoning with salt to taste. Bring to simmering point, cover and cook for about 25 minutes, until the rice is tender.

Cook's Tip

Serve this dish with a simple side salad accompaniment, naan bread and yogurt.

118 | Coriander Beef with Aubergine

Preparation time
20 minutes

Cooking time
about 2¼ hours

Serves 6

Calories
500 per portion

You will need
75 ml/3 fl oz oil
2 onions, finely sliced
2.5 cm/1 inch piece root ginger,
  chopped
3 garlic cloves, chopped
3 tablespoons ground coriander
½ teaspoon hot chilli powder
1 kg/2 lb lean boneless beef, cut
  into 4-cm/1½-inch cubes
475 ml/16 fl oz beef stock
1 large aubergine, cut into
  4-cm/1½-inch cubes
675 g/1½ lb tomatoes, chopped
1 (400-g/14-oz) can chick peas,
  drained
salt and pepper
1 teaspoon garam masala (see
  Cook's Tip recipe 67)

Heat the oil, add the onion and cook for 10 minutes until tender. Add the ginger, garlic, coriander and chilli powder, then cook for 2 minutes. Stir in the beef and brown for 5 minutes, turning frequently.

Add the stock, bring to the boil, reduce the heat, cover and simmer for 1½ hours.

Stir in the aubergine, cover and simmer for 20 minutes. Add the tomatoes and chick peas, cover and simmer for a further 10 minutes, then season to taste with salt and pepper. Stir in the garam masala and serve at once.

Cook's Tip

Sprinkling aubergine cubes with salt draws out any bitter juices and also prevents the aubergine absorbing too much oil. Rinse thoroughly through, or the cubes will taste salty.

119 | *Sweet and Sour Beef Stew*

Preparation time
20 minutes

Cooking time
about 1¼ hours

Serves 4–6

Calories
500–360 per portion

You will need
1 kg/2 lb boneless stewing beef, cut into 5-cm/2-inch cubes
1 large onion, thinly sliced
4 green chillies, seeded and thinly sliced
2 thin slices root ginger, crushed
2 large garlic cloves, crushed
2 tablespoons oil
1 teaspoon laos powder (see Cook's Tip recipe 170)
475 ml/16 fl oz beef stock
100 ml/4 fl oz ketjap manis (see Cook's Tip)
4 tablespoons red wine vinegar
2 teaspoons sugar
salt

Mix the meat, onion, chillies, ginger, garlic, oil and laos powder in a large pan. Place over medium high heat and cook for 5–10 minutes, stirring occasionally, until the meat has browned on all sides.

Stir in the remaining ingredients, bring to the boil, stirring frequently, then lower the heat and simmer for 1 hour or until the sauce is reduced to a thick glaze.

Transfer the stew to a heated serving dish and serve with boiled rice.

120 | *Minced Beef on Skewers*

Preparation time
20 minutes, plus 30 minutes chilling time

Cooking time
about 15 minutes

Serves 4–6

Calories
500–360 per portion

You will need
675 g/1½ lb minced beef
2 large onions, chopped
4 garlic cloves, chopped
75 g/3 oz breadcrumbs
3 tablespoons chopped fresh coriander leaves
2 teaspoons garam masala (see Cook's Tip recipe 67)
2 teaspoons black pepper
1½ teaspoons poppy seeds
1½ teaspoons sesame seeds
½ teaspoon chilli powder
1½ teaspoons salt
2 eggs, beaten

Pass the beef, onions and garlic through the finest blade of a mincer, or work in a food processor. Knead well then mix in the remaining ingredients. Chill for 30 minutes.

Press the mixture on to 6 skewers, in sausage shapes about 10 cm/4 inches long (there should be enough mixture to make 12 shapes, 2 on each skewer). Barbecue or grill under or over a moderate heat until cooked, turning frequently. Serve hot.

Cook's Tip

Ketjap manis is an Indonesian sweetened soy sauce. To make your own, bring 150 g/5 oz demerara sugar and 250 ml/8 fl oz water to a simmer, stirring constantly. Increase the heat until the syrup reaches 100 C/200 F on a sugar thermometer. Reduce the heat to low, stir in 7 tablespoons black treacle, 1 teaspoon grated root ginger, ½ teaspoon ground coriander and freshly ground black pepper. Simmer for 3 minutes.

Cook's Tip

Remove items from skewers with the prongs of a fork. Remember to protect your hand with a double-thick tea-towel if the skewers are hot from the grill or barbecue.

121 | Deep-Fried Beef Slices

Preparation time
10 minutes, plus 20–25 minutes marinating time

Cooking time
3–5 minutes

Serves 4–6

Calories
380–250 per portion

You will need
4 spring onions, chopped
pinch of salt
1 tablespoon dry sherry
2.5 cm/1 inch piece root ginger, chopped
1 tablespoon chilli sauce
1 chilli, seeded and chopped
450 g/1 lb rump steak
oil for deep frying

For the batter
4 tablespoons plain flour
pinch of salt
1 egg
3–4 tablespoons water

Put the spring onions, salt, sherry, ginger, chilli sauce and chilli in a bowl and mix well. Cut the steak into thin slices and add to the marinade. Toss well to coat and leave to marinate for 20–25 minutes.

Meanwhile, make the batter. Sift the flour and salt into a bowl, break in the egg and beat well, adding sufficient water to make a smooth batter.

Heat the oil in a wok or deep-frier. Dip the steak slices into the batter and deep-fry until golden. Drain on absorbent kitchen paper. Serve at once.

122 | Beef Curry with Potatoes

Preparation time
20 minutes

Cooking time
about 1½–1¾ hours

Serves 4

Calories
540 per portion

You will need
4 tablespoons oil
2 onions, finely chopped
2 garlic cloves, chopped
1 teaspoon chilli powder
1 tablespoon ground cumin
1½ tablespoons ground coriander
2.5 cm/1 inch piece root ginger, finely chopped
675 g/1½ lb stewing steak, cubed
2 tablespoons tomato purée
salt
350 g/12 oz new potatoes, scraped and halved if large
4 green chillies

Heat the oil in a large pan, add the onions and fry until lightly coloured. Add the garlic, chilli powder, cumin, coriander and ginger and cook gently for 5 minutes, stirring occasionally.

Add the beef and cook, stirring, until browned all over. Add the tomato purée, salt to taste and just enough water to cover the meat; stir very well. Bring to the boil, cover and simmer for about 1 hour or until the meat is almost tender. Add the potatoes and whole chillies and simmer until the potatoes are cooked.

Cook's Tip

This dish looks especially good if garnished with lemon wedges and fresh coriander leaves. Serve with soy sauce handed separately.

Cook's Tip

Leftover amounts of tomato purée from a tin can be frozen in an ice-cube tray and stored for further use.

123 | *Beef with Hot Salad*

Preparation time
10 minutes

Cooking time
5–8 minutes

Serves 4

Calories
250 per portion

You will need
450 g/1 lb fillet steak
1 large onion, sliced into rings
2 chillies
2 garlic cloves, crushed
½ teaspoon sugar
½ teaspoon soy sauce
juice of 1 lime or lemon
1 teaspoon chopped mint

Cut the beef along the grain into strips about 6 cm/2½ inches long, 2.5 cm/1 inch wide and 1 cm/½ inch thick. Put the onion rings and chillies on a skewer and grill until soft. Remove from the skewer, then mash together.

Grill the beef until just cooked to taste, then mix with the mashed mixture. Add the remaining ingredients and mix. Place on a warmed serving plate and serve surrounded with a selection of fresh seasonal vegetables such as cucumbers, tomatoes, Chinese cabbage, beansprouts, etc.

124 | *Japanese 'Roast' Beef*

Preparation time
about 20 minutes

Cooking time
about 10 minutes

Serves 4

Calories
400 per portion

You will need
675 g/1½ lb sirloin of beef
1 garlic clove, sliced
100 ml/4 fl oz soy sauce
100 ml/4 fl oz sake (rice wine)
1½ teaspoons sugar
2 spring onions, finely chopped
2.5 cm/1 inch piece root ginger, grated
watercress sprigs, to garnish

Put the beef in a deep pan with the garlic, soy sauce, sake and sugar. Cover the joint with a small upturned plate then cover the pan, place over a high heat and bring to the boil. Lower the heat and simmer for 10 minutes, shaking the pan to prevent the meat sticking.

Remove from the heat and leave to cool in the liquid until cold. Slice the meat thinly, then arrange on individual serving plates with the spring onions and ginger. The juice is served separately in small bowls and the meat is garnished with watercress sprigs.

Cook's Tip

Sirloin, rump or even topside of beef can be used instead of fillet steak for a more economical meal – after slicing the meat treat it with a meat tenderizer, then leave for about 10 minutes before cooking. In Thailand, where **this dish originated, papaya peel is used to make the meat tender. The flavour of this dish is greatly improved if the onion, chillies and beef are grilled over glowing charcoal rather than using the conventional grill.**

Cook's Tip

To eat, each person mixes a little spring onion and ginger with some of the sauce, then dips a slice of meat into it before eating. If you prefer, mustard can be substituted for the ginger and spring onion.

125 | *Korean Spiced Raw Beef*

Preparation time
20–30 minutes

Serves 4

Calories
420 per portion with egg yolks (340 per portion without egg yolks)

You will need
450 g/1 lb beef, fillet or rump
2 teaspoons sugar
2 teaspoons sesame seeds
1 tablespoon sesame oil
1 tablespoon crushed garlic
salt
4 egg yolks (optional)

For the garnish
2 small hard pears, peeled and cut into strips
12 diagonal slices of cucumber, cut into strips
parsley sprigs (optional)
carrot slices (optional)

Cut the meat into very thin slices no more than 3 mm/⅛ inch thick, then cut the slices into matchstick strips. Place in a bowl with the remaining ingredients, except the egg yolks. Mix together and divide into 4 portions.

Divide the pear and cucumber strips equally between 4 individual serving plates, arranging them in separate piles. Place the meat mixture on top. If using egg yolks, mould the mixture into a neat bowl-shape and put an egg yolk in each hollow. Garnish with parsley sprigs and carrot flower slices if liked. Serve raw.

126 | *Szechuan Hot Shredded Beef*

Preparation time
10–15 minutes

Cooking time
about 10 minutes

Serves 4–6

Calories
400–270 per portion

You will need
450 g/1 lb rump or frying steak
2 tablespoons cornflour
salt
3 tablespoons oil
4 spring onions, chopped
2 celery sticks, sliced diagonally
4 carrots, sliced diagonally
2 tablespoons soy sauce
1 tablespoon hoisin sauce
3 teaspoons chilli sauce
2 tablespoons dry sherry

Cut the steak into 5-cm/2-inch long thin slices. Toss the steak in the cornflour and season with salt to taste.

Heat the oil in a wok or frying pan, add the spring onions and fry for 1 minute. Add the meat slices and cook for 4 minutes, stirring until the meat is lightly browned. Add the celery and carrots and cook for 2 minutes. Stir in the soy, hoisin and chilli sauces and the sherry, bring to the boil and cook for 1 minute.

Arrange on a warmed serving dish and serve at once.

Cook's Tip

This is the Korean version of Steak Tartare. The egg yolk is broken at the table and mixed with the beef, pear and cucumber.
   Use either chopsticks or a fork for mixing and eating.

Cook's Tip

Hoisin sauce is a thick, brownish-red soy-based sauce that is used as a condiment and in cooked Chinese dishes.

127 | Fried Beef with Scrambled Egg

Preparation time
15 minutes

Cooking time
5–10 minutes

Serves 4

Calories
450 per portion

You will need
½ teaspoon grated root ginger
1 tablespoon dry sherry
1 teaspoon sugar
2 teaspoons soy sauce
1 tablespoon cornflour
5 tablespoons oil
225 g/8 oz beef fillet, thinly sliced
    across the grain into bite-sized
    pieces
4 large eggs
salt and pepper
oil for deep frying
1 spring onion, chopped

Mix the ginger with the sherry, sugar, soy sauce, corn-flour and 1 tablespoon of the oil. Add the beef and leave to marinate while preparing the eggs.

Beat the eggs with 1 tablespoon of the oil and salt and pepper to taste until light and fluffy.

Heat the oil to 160 C/325 F, then deep fry the beef for a few seconds until the colour changes. Drain.

Heat the remaining 3 tablespoons of oil in a pan. Add the deep-fried beef and eggs and stir-fry briskly over a high heat. Add the spring onion and stir for a few seconds until the eggs are cooked. Serve at once.

128 | Stir-Fried Sesame Beef

Preparation time
20 minutes, including marinating time

Cooking time
6 minutes

Serves 4

Calories
350 per portion

You will need
350 g/12 oz rump steak
1 tablespoon light soy sauce
1 tablespoon dark soy sauce
1 tablespoon soft light brown
    sugar
1 teaspoon sesame oil
1 tablespoon dry sherry
2 tablespoons white sesame
    seeds
2 tablespoons oil
1 garlic clove, thinly sliced
2 celery sticks, sliced diagonally
2 carrots, sliced diagonally
50 g/2 oz button mushrooms,
    sliced

Cut the steak into thin slices, across the grain. Combine the soy sauces, sugar, sesame oil and sherry. Toss in the meat and leave to marinate for 15 minutes.

Fry the sesame seeds until they are golden brown. Heat the oil in a wok or frying pan, add the garlic, celery and carrots and stir-fry briskly for 1 minute; remove from the pan. Increase the heat, add the beef and stir-fry for about 3 minutes, until well browned. Return the vegetables to the wok, add the mushrooms and cook for a further 30 seconds. Sprinkle with the sesame seeds and serve at once.

Cook's Tip

A Chinese meal is rather like a buffet. Platters are used for each dish and everyone is expected to eat from all of them. Small rice bowls on plates are provided as a stop between platter and mouth.

A properly planned Chinese meal consists of one meat dish such as the one above, one fowl dish and one fish dish accompanied by vegetables and rice or noodles.

Cook's Tip

An easy way to slice mushrooms is to use an egg slicer.

129 | *Stir-Fried Orange Beef*

Preparation time
20 minutes, including marinating time

Cooking time
7 minutes

Serves 4

Calories
370 per portion

You will need
350 g/12 oz rump steak
2 teaspoons sesame oil
2 tablespoons dark soy sauce
1 tablespoon dry sherry
2.5 cm/1 inch piece root ginger, finely chopped
2 teaspoons cornflour
4 tablespoons oil
2 dried red chillies, crumbled
shredded rind of 1 orange
pinch of salt
½ teaspoon roasted Szechuan peppercorns, finely ground
1 teaspoon light soft brown sugar

Cut the beef into thin slices 5 cm/2 inches long, cutting against the grain.

Combine half the sesame oil and soy sauce, the sherry, ginger and cornflour, add the meat and toss until well coated. Leave to marinate for 15 minutes; drain well.

Heat the oil and quickly brown the meat on all sides for 2 minutes; drain on kitchen paper. Pour off all but 1 tablespoon oil from the pan. Heat the pan, add the chillies and stir-fry for 30 seconds. Return the meat, add the orange rind, salt, pepper, sugar and remaining soy sauce. Stir-fry for 4 minutes, sprinkle with the remaining sesame oil and serve at once.

130 | *Thai Beef Curry*

Preparation time
15 minutes

Cooking time
2 hours

Serves 4

Calories
440 per portion

You will need
750 ml/1¼ pints thick coconut milk
675 g/1½ lb stewing steak, cubed
salt
2 chillies, finely sliced
2 tablespoons fish or soy sauce
3 lime leaves (optional)

For the spice paste
4 garlic cloves
2 small onions, quartered
3–6 small dried red chillies
1 teaspoon grated lemon rind
1 teaspoon laos powder
1 piece root ginger
1 tablespoon ground coriander
1 teaspoon ground cumin
1 teaspoon turmeric

Bring 600 ml/1 pint of the coconut milk to simmering point in a pan. Add the beef and salt to taste, cover and simmer for 1–1½ hours until the meat is tender. Lift out the beef and set aside. Meanwhile, place all the ingredients for the spice paste in a liquidizer or food processor and work until smooth.

Pour the remaining coconut milk into a second pan; stir in the spice paste and cook, stirring for 15 minutes or until the mixture is dry and well fried. Gradually add the coconut milk from the first pan and bring to simmering point. Add the beef, chillies, fish or soy sauce and lime leaves, if using. Cook for 10–15 minutes until the sauce is thick. Serve at once.

Cook's Tip

This recipe originates from the northern part of China. This area stretches from the Yangtze river to the Great Wall of China, and embraces the culinary styles of both Peking and Shantung. It may be garnished with orange slices and parsley sprigs if liked.

Cook's Tip

Thai curries are fiery and much hotter than the Indian curries from which they derive. They use the small shiny, ferocious chillies which are available in the West – use them at your peril!

131 | *Stir-Fried Chilli Beef*

Preparation time
2 minutes

Cooking time
3½ minutes

Serves 4

Calories
340 per portion

You will need
450 g/1 lb rump steak
salt
2 tablespoons oil
2 dried red chillies
2 garlic cloves, sliced
1 piece root ginger, shredded
4 spring onions, shredded
2 tablespoons dark soy sauce
2 tablespoons light soy sauce
2 tablespoons dry sherry
2 green chillies, seeded and chopped

Cut the steak into thin slices, across the grain, and season well with salt.

Heat the oil in a wok or deep frying pan, add the red chillies and fry for 1 minute. Remove from the pan. Increase the heat, add the steak and stir-fry for 1 minute, until browned. Add the garlic, ginger and spring onions and cook for 30 seconds. Pour over the soy sauces and sherry, add the green chillies and cook for a further minute. Serve at once.

132 | *Beef with Plums*

Preparation time
6 minutes

Cooking time
8 minutes

Serves 4

Calories
220 per portion

You will need
1 tablespoon oil
1 onion, thinly sliced
1 garlic clove, crushed
2–3 pieces beef, cut into thin slivers
2–3 dessert plums, stoned and cut into slices
2–3 mushrooms, sliced
1 tablespoon sherry
2 teaspoons soft brown sugar
1 tablespoon soy sauce
2 teaspoons cornflour blended with 2 tablespoons water
chopped spring onion tops to garnish

Heat the oil in a large frying pan, add the onion and fry for 2 minutes. Stir in the garlic and meat strips and stir-fry over a high heat for 2 minutes. Lower the heat and add the plums and mushrooms. Continue to stir-fry for 1 minute, then stir in the sherry, sugar, soy sauce and blended cornflour. Cook, stirring, until the sauce has thickened. Serve at once, garnished with chopped spring onion tops.

Cook's Tip

Chillies are used extensively in the dishes of western China. Fresh red chillies are milder than the green ones, because they become sweeter as they ripen. Dried red chillies are used to season the oil for stir-fried dishes. The seeds are often left in, which makes the dish very hot and spicy; they may be removed if a less hot dish is preferred.

Cook's Tip

Try serving this quickly cooked dish with wholewheat tagliatelle or noodles and a green vegetable such as broccoli, spinach or French beans.

133 | Beef Rendang

Preparation time
20 minutes

Cooking time
1½–2 hours

Serves 4

Calories
470 per portion

You will need
4 teaspoons chilli powder
4 small onions, chopped
4 garlic cloves
5 cm/2 inch piece root ginger, chopped
1 teaspoon turmeric
1 tablespoon ground coriander
1 teaspoon ground cumin
1 teaspoon grated lemon rind
900 ml/1½ pints thick coconut milk
100 ml/4 fl oz tamarind water (see Cook's Tip recipe 11)
1 teaspoon sugar
1 teaspoon salt
675 g/1½ lb rump steak, cubed
4 curry leaves

Place the chilli powder, onions, garlic, ginger, turmeric, coriander, cumin and lemon rind in a liquidizer or food processor and work until smooth. Place in a large pan, stir in the coconut milk, tamarind water, sugar and salt. Mix well, add the beef and curry leaves and bring to the boil. Lower the heat and cook, uncovered, stirring frequently for about 30 minutes or until the sauce is thick.

Reduce the heat to low and continue cooking for about 1–1½ hours, until the curry is dry and deep brown. Stir frequently and be careful not to let it burn. Serve hot with rice and garnished with lime twists if liked.

134 | Peking Noodles

Preparation time
10 minutes

Cooking time
6 minutes

Serves 4–6

Calories
600–410 per portion

You will need
450 g/1 lb fresh wholewheat noodles
1 tablespoon oil
1 onion, thinly sliced
2.5 cm/1 inch piece root ginger, chopped
1 garlic clove, crushed
about 225 g/8 oz lean minced beef
1 tablespoon soy sauce
2 tablespoons sherry
2–3 teaspoons sugar
1 tablespoon cornflour blended with 4 tablespoons water

Cook the noodles in a large pan of boiling salted water for about 3 minutes. Drain and keep warm.

Heat the oil in a large frying pan, add the onion, ginger and garlic and stir-fry for just over 1 minute. Add the beef and stir-fry until evenly browned. Stir in the soy sauce, sherry and sugar and continue stir-frying for 2 minutes. Stir in the blended cornflour and cook, stirring until thickened.

Divide the noodles between warmed individual plates and spoon the sauce over them. Serve at once.

Cook's Tip

Rendang is a famous Indonesian dry beef curry. Blistering hot in its native Sumatra – something you can alter by reducing the number of chillies – it is a dish which requires careful cooking, particularly in the last stages when the meat must turn a dark brown without burning. This curry improves with keeping, so ideally make a day before required.

Cook's Tip

Serve Peking Noodles with a salad of shredded white cabbage, cucumber strips, sliced radishes, chopped beansprouts and grated carrot, scattered over the noodles if liked.

135 | Lamb Korma

Preparation time
15 minutes

Cooking time
about 1½ hours

Serves 4

Calories
500 per portion

You will need
5 tablespoons oil
6 cardamoms
6 cloves
6 peppercorns
2.5 cm/1inch cinnamon stick
675 g/1½ lb boned leg of lamb,
  cubed
6 small onions, chopped
2 garlic cloves, chopped
5 cm/2 inch piece root ginger,
  chopped
2 tablespoons ground coriander
2 teaspoons ground cumin
1 teaspoon chilli powder
salt
150 g/5 oz natural yogurt
1 teaspoon garam masala

Heat 4 tablespoons of the oil in a pan, add the carda-moms, cloves, peppercorns and cinnamon and fry for 1 minute. Add the lamb, a few pieces at a time, and fry until browned on all sides; transfer to a dish. Remove the whole spices and discard.

Add the remaining oil to the pan and fry the onions, gar-lic and ginger for 5 minutes, then add the coriander, cumin, chilli powder and salt to taste and cook for 5 minutes, stirring frequently. Gradually stir in the yogurt. Return the meat and any juices and sufficient water to just cover the meat. Bring to simmering point, cover and cook for about 1 hour until tender.

Sprinkle on the garam masala and cook for 1 minute. Serve at once.

Cook's Tip

Lamb Korma is one of the mildest of curries, using a subtle blend of spices with yogurt. Serve with a lentil and spinach dish such as Dhal Sag (recipe 26) and boiled rice.

136 | Roghan Ghosht

Preparation time
20 minutes

Cooking time
about 1¼ hours

Serves 4

Calories
650 per portion

You will need
4 tablespoons oil
2 onions, finely chopped
675 g/1½ lb boned leg of lamb,
  cubed
300 g/10 oz natural yogurt
2 garlic cloves
2.5 cm/1 inch piece root ginger,
  chopped
2 green chillies
1 tablespoon coriander seeds
1 teaspoon cumin seeds
1 teaspoon chopped fresh mint
  leaves
1 teaspoon chopped coriander
  leaves
6 cardamoms
6 cloves
2.5 cm/1 inch cinnamon stick
100 g/4 oz flaked almonds

Heat 2 tablespoons of the oil in a pan, add 1 onion and fry until golden. Add the lamb and 175 g/6 oz of the yogurt; stir well, cover and simmer for 20 minutes.

Place the garlic, ginger, chillies, coriander seeds, cumin, mint, coriander and 2–3 tablespoons of the yogurt in a liquidizer or food processor and work to a paste.

Heat the remaining oil in a large pan, add the carda-moms, cloves and cinnamon and fry for 1 minute. Add the second onion, prepared paste and fry for 5 minutes, stirring constantly. Add the lamb and yogurt mixture and salt to taste. Bring to simmering point, cover and cook for 30 minutes. Add the almonds and cook for a further 15 minutes. Serve hot.

Cook's Tip

If liked, serve the curry sprinkled with chopped fresh mint and garnished with fresh mint leaves. Serve with boiled rice and selection of chutneys and relishes.

137 | Lamb Curry with Yogurt

Preparation time
15 minutes

Cooking time
about 1¼ hours

Serves 4

Calories
450 per portion

You will need
4 tablespoons oil
3 onions, chopped
6 cardamoms
5 cm/2 inch cinnamon stick
1½ tablespoons ground coriander
2 tablespoons ground cumin
½ teaspoon turmeric
½ teaspoon ground cloves
1–2 teaspoons chilli powder
½ teaspoon grated nutmeg
2 tablespoons water
1 tablespoon paprika
300 g/10 oz natural yogurt
675 g/1½ lb boned leg of lamb,
    cubed
1 large tomato, skinned and
    chopped
salt

Heat the oil in a large pan, add the onions, cardamoms and cinnamon and fry until the onions are golden. Stir in the coriander, cumin, turmeric, cloves, chilli powder and nutmeg. Fry until dry, then add the water and cook, stirring, for 5 minutes, adding a little more water if needed.

Add the paprika and slowly stir in the yogurt. Add the lamb, tomato and salt to taste and mix well. Bring to simmering point, cover and cook for 1 hour or until the meat is tender.

138 | Dry Lamb Curry

Preparation time
10–15 minutes

Cooking time
about 50 minutes

Serves 4

Calories
450 per portion

You will need
3 tablespoons oil
225 g/8 oz onions, finely chopped
6 cloves
6 cardamoms
2.5 cm/1 inch cinnamon stick
2 green chillies, finely chopped
675 g/1½ lb boned leg of lamb,
    cut into strips
2 teaspoons ground coriander
1 teaspoon ground cumin
300 g/10 oz natural yogurt
2 tablespoons chopped fresh
    coriander leaves
3 curry leaves
salt
1 teaspoon garam masala

Heat the oil in a pan, add the onions and fry until soft. Add the cloves, cardamoms and cinnamon and fry for 1 minute, then add the chillies and lamb. Fry for a further 10 minutes, turning the lamb to brown on all sides.

Add the remaining ingredients, except garam masala, seasoning with salt to taste. Stir well, bring to simmering point and cook, uncovered, for 40 minutes until the meat is tender and the liquid has evaporated. Stir in the garam masala and serve.

Cook's Tip

Curry comes from the Tamil word for a relish. It has been used as a convenient shorthand in the West for dishes, particularly stews, made of meat, fish or vegetables, cooked with spices and served with rice or Indian breads. True curries were born in southern India. They belong to those regions where rice is the staple food and where the climate is hot and humid.

Cook's Tip

Curry making becomes easy if, before starting to cook, you assemble the required ingredients: measure out spices and seasonings and put them in separate piles; chop or slice the other foodstuffs before starting.

139 | Lamb Kebab

Preparation time
10 minutes, plus
overnight chilling time

Cooking time
10 minutes

Serves 4

Calories
450 per portion

You will need
300 g/10 oz natural yogurt
1 tablespoon ground coriander
½ teaspoon chilli powder
1 tablespoon oil
salt
675 g/1½ lb boned leg of lamb,
    cubed
4 onions
2 red peppers
4 tomatoes
2 tablespoons finely chopped
    fresh coriander leaves

Put the yogurt, coriander, chilli, oil and salt to taste in a large bowl. Add the meat, mix well, cover and chill overnight in the refrigerator.

Cut the onion into quarters and separate the layers. Core and seed the peppers and cut into squares and cut the tomatoes in half.

Thread the onion, lamb and red pepper alternately on to 8 skewers, beginning and ending each kebab with a tomato half. Cook under a preheated hot grill for about 10 minutes, turning frequently and basting with any remaining marinade as necessary. Sprinkle with chopped coriander to serve.

140 | Malabar Lamb Curry

Preparation time
10 minutes

Cooking time
1 hour

Serves 4

Calories
470 per portion

You will need
3 tablespoons oil or ghee
2 onions, finely chopped
1 teaspoon turmeric
1 tablespoon ground coriander
1 teaspoon ground cumin
2 teaspoons chilli powder
½ teaspoon ground cloves
12 curry leaves
675 g/1½ lb boned leg of lamb,
    cubed
1 tablespoon coarsely grated fresh
    cococnut
300 ml/½ pint water
1 teaspoon salt

Heat the oil or ghee in a pan, add the onions and fry until golden. Stir in the turmeric, coriander, cumin, chilli powder, cloves and curry leaves and fry for 1–2 minutes.

Add the meat and coconut and fry, stirring, until well browned. Pour in the water and add the salt. Cover and simmer for 45 minutes or until the lamb is tender. Turn on to a warmed serving dish and serve hot.

Cook's Tip

Serve the kebabs with a finger bowl – make it effective by adding a few drops of lemon juice and make it look decorative by floating a few flower heads on the surface.

Cook's Tip

This is a southern Indian curry which is delicious served with rice, poppadoms, chutneys and a Pineapple Raita: beat a little salt and sugar into a bowl of natural yogurt, stir in some pineapple chunks and a finely chopped green chilli.

141 | Stir-Fried Lamb with Noodles

Preparation time
15 minutes, including
soaking time

Cooking time
8 minutes

Serves 4–6

Calories
330–220 per portion

You will need
100 g/4 oz cellophane noodles
1 tablespoon oil
3 spring onions, chopped
2.5 cm/1 inch piece root ginger,
  chopped
2 garlic cloves, sliced
2 celery sticks, chopped
450 g/1 lb very lean lamb, thinly
  sliced
1 red pepper, cored, seeded and
  sliced
2 tablespoons light soy sauce
2 tablespoons dry sherry
150 ml/¼ pint stock
2 teaspoons sesame oil

Soak the noodles in warm water for about 10 minutes; drain.

Heat the oil in a wok or frying pan, add the spring onions, ginger and garlic and stir-fry for 1 minute. Add the celery and lamb and cook for 2 minutes. Add the red pepper, soy sauce and sherry and bring to the boil. Stir in the stock and noddles and simmer for 5 minutes. Sprinkle with the sesame oil.

Serve at once, garnished as shown if liked.

142 | Lamb with Extra Onions

Preparation time
15 minutes

Cooking time
about 1–1¼ hours

Serves 4–6

Calories
700–480 per portion

You will need
675 g/1½ lb boneless shoulder of
  lamb, cubed
5 large onions
100 g/4 oz ghee
6 garlic cloves, peeled
1 piece root ginger
1 tablespoon chilli powder
2 teaspoons ground coriander
2 teaspoons ground cumin
2 teaspoons black pepper
1½ teaspoons turmeric
2 teaspoons salt
350 g/12 oz natural yogurt
300 ml/½ pint beef stock
6 green chillies, chopped
1 tablespoon fenugreek seeds
2 tablespoons chopped fresh mint

Place the lamb in a bowl. Purée 1 onion in a liquidizer or food processor and add to the lamb.

Heat the ghee, add the lamb mixture and fry on all sides. Slice the remaining onions, garlic and ginger. Remove the lamb with a slotted spoon and set aside. Add the sliced onions, garlic and ginger and fry gently for 4–5 minutes. Meanwhile, mix the ground spices and salt with the yogurt. Add to the pan, increase the heat and add the lamb, stirring constantly. Add the stock, bring to the boil, cover and simmer for 40 minutes.

Add the chillies, fenugreek and mint and simmer for a further 5–10 minutes. Serve hot.

Cook's Tip

Use lean boneless leg of lamb or lamb neck fillets for this dish – removing any visible fat and cutting the flesh in thin slices.

Cook's Tip

This recipe is called Goscht Dopiaza in Indian, which is roughly translated as 'meat with double onions' since the Hindu word for onion is piaz and the word for two is do (pronounced dough). Onions form a crucial part of virtually all Indian curry dishes and, in fact, many Indians regard onions as vegetables in themselves.

143 | Royal Lamb Curry

Preparation time
15 minutes, plus 2
hours marinating time

Cooking time
about 1¼ hours

Serves 4

Calories
900 per portion

You will need
1 kg/2 lb boneless lamb, cubed
juice of 1 lemon
225 g/8 oz natural yogurt
75 g/3 oz ghee
2 onions, sliced
4 garlic cloves, sliced
2.5 cm/1 inch piece root ginger,
 sliced
7.5-cm/3-inch cinnamon stick
10 cloves
10 cardamoms
2 teaspoons ground coriander
2 teaspoons ground cumin
2 teaspoons chilli powder
1 teaspoon turmeric
1 teaspoon black pepper
1½ teaspoons salt
100 g/4 oz blanched almonds
50 g/2 oz shelled pistachios
150 ml/¼ pint single cream

Mix the lamb with the lemon juice and yogurt and leave to marinate for 2 hours.

Heat the ghee, add the onions, garlic and ginger and fry for 5 minutes. Add the cinnamon, cloves and cardamoms; fry for 1 minute. Add the remaining spices and salt and pepper and cook for 2–3 minutes. Add the lamb and marinade, then stir in 300 ml/½ pint boiling water. Stir in half of the almonds, cover and simmer for 50 minutes.

Add the remaining almonds, pistachios and cream and simmer for 5–10 minutes without boiling. Serve hot.

144 | Spiced Leg of Lamb

Preparation time
15 minutes, plus 3
hours or overnight
marinating time

Cooking time
2½ hours

Oven temperature
180 C, 350 F, gas 4

Serves 4

Calories
530 per portion

You will need
1.75–2.5 kg/4–5 lb leg of lamb
6 garlic cloves, crushed
6 slices root ginger, shredded
2 onions, thinly sliced
1.2 litres/2 pints stock
5 tablespoons soy sauce
3 tablespoons soy bean paste or
 hoisin sauce
2 tablespoons dried chilli pepper
 or chilli sauce
½ teaspoon Chinese 5-spice
 powder
2 tablespoons sugar
300 ml/½ pint red wine
1 chicken stock cube

Place all the ingredients except the lamb in a saucepan and simmer gently for 45 minutes.

Place the lamb in another pan, pour over the sauce, bring to the boil, then simmer gently for 1½ hours, turning every 30 minutes. Remove from the heat and allow to cool in the sauce, then leave to marinate for a further 3 hours or overnight.

About 1 hour before serving, place the lamb in a roasting tin and cook for 1 hour. Slice the lamb into bite-sized pieces and serve hot or cold.

Cook's Tip

This rich and exotic curry was
created for the great Mogul
Emperors. Varak or silver leaf
is often used to decorate it. It
is safe to eat and aluminium
foil should not be used as a
substitute.

Cook's Tip

Lamb was introduced to
northern China by the
Mongols, who invaded China
and set up a dynasty which
ruled from 1279 to 1368. This
is one of a number of dishes
adapted by the Chinese to suit
their tastes.

Serve this dish hot or cold
with dips such as hoisin
sauce, soy sauce and sherry
mixed together, or soy sauce
mixed with a little vinegar.

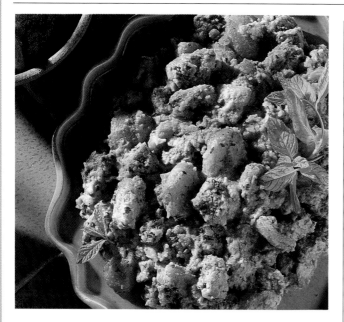

149 | *Apricot and Lamb Curry*

Preparation time
20 minutes, plus overnight soaking time

Cooking time
1 hour

Serves 4

Calories
700 per portion

You will need
4 onions, 2 quartered and 2 chopped
2 garlic cloves
½–1 teaspoon small dried red chillies
50 g/2 oz blanched almonds
1 tablespoon ground coriander
3 tablespoons oil
5 cm/2 inch cinnamon stick
6 cardamoms
8 cloves
675 g/1½ lb boned leg of lamb, cubed
275 g/10 oz natural yogurt
225 g/8 oz dried apricots, soaked overnight
salt
1 tablespoon chopped mint leaves

Put the quartered onions, garlic, chillies, almonds and coriander in a liquidizer or food processor and work to a smooth paste.

Heat the oil, add the cinnamon, cardamoms and cloves and fry for a few seconds. When they change colour remove and discard. Add the remaining onions to the pan and fry until soft. Add the prepared paste and fry for 3–4 minutes. Add the lamb and fry, stirring for 5 minutes. Stir in the yogurt, a spoonful at a time, then the drained apricots and salt to taste. Simmer, partially covered, for 40 minutes until tender. Stir in the mint and serve at once.

150 | *Stir-Fried Garlic Lamb*

Preparation time
20 minutes, including marinating time

Cooking time
5 minutes

Serves 4

Calories
220 per portion

You will need
350 g/12 oz lamb fillet
2 tablespoons dry sherry
2 tablespoons light soy sauce
1 tablespoon dark soy sauce
1 teaspoon sesame oil
2 tablespoons oil
6 garlic cloves, thinly sliced
2.5 cm/1 inch piece root ginger, chopped
1 leek, thinly sliced diagonally
4 spring onions, chopped

Cut the lamb into thin slices across the grain. Mix the sherry with the soy sauces and sesame oil. Add the lamb and toss to coat. Leave to marinate for 15 minutes then drain, reserving the marinade.

Heat the oil in a wok or deep frying pan, add the meat and about 2 teaspoons of the marinade and fry briskly for about 2 minutes until well browned. Add the garlic, ginger, leek and spring onions and fry for a further 3 minutes. Serve at once.

Cook's Tip

Apricots go especially well with lamb but must be of the best quality with a bright colour and sharp taste; pallid sweet fruit will add nothing to the dish.

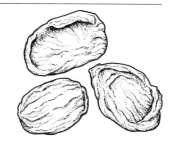

Cook's Tip

This recipe originates from northern China. Because of the harshness of its climate, it is difficult to obtain fresh vegetables in this area throughout much of the year. Many of the recipes therefore rely heavily on garlic, spring onions, leeks, sesame seeds, oil and sweet bean sauce.

151 | Steamed Stuffed Aubergines

Preparation time
15 minutes

Cooking time
about 1 hour

Serves 4–6

Calories
190–130 per portion

You will need
1 tablespoon oil
2 garlic cloves, crushed
2.5 cm/1 inch piece root ginger, chopped
4 spring onions, chopped
2 red or green chillies, seeded and chopped
225 g/8 oz minced pork
2 tablespoons soy sauce
2 tablespoons dry sherry
4 medium aubergines
50 g/2 oz peeled prawns

Heat the oil in a wok or deep frying pan, add the garlic, ginger and spring onions and stir-fry for 1 minute. Increase the heat, add the chillies and pork and cook for 2 minutes. Stir in the soy sauce and sherry and cook for 10 minutes.

Meanwhile, halve the aubergines lengthways, carefully scoop out the flesh and chop finely. Add the flesh to the pan and cook for 10 minutes. Stir in the prawns and cook for 1 minute.

Blanch the aubergine shells in boiling water for 1 minute. Drain and stuff with the meat mixture. Place in a dish in a steamer and steam for 25–30 minutes, then serve at once.

152 | Crispy Barbecued Pork

Preparation time
10 minutes, plus 1¾ hours standing time

Cooking time
about 1¼ hours

Oven temperature
230 C, 450 F, gas 8
then
200 C, 400 F, gas 6

Serves 6–8

Calories
650–500 per portion

You will need
1.5 kg/3 lb lean belly of pork, in one piece
salt
1 tablespoon soy sauce
1 teaspoon Chinese 5-spice powder

Pour a kettleful of boiling water over the skin of the pork; drain and dry. Rub the pork with salt and leave to dry for 45 minutes.

Score the skin of the pork in a diamond pattern. Pierce the meat with a skewer in several places. Rub the soy sauce and 5-spice powder into the pork. Cover and leave to stand for 1 hour.

Place the pork, skin side up, in a roasting tin and roast at the higher temperature for 20 minutes. Lower the heat and continue to roast for 50–55 minutes, or until the pork is tender and the skin is crisp. Slice to serve.

Cook's Tip

Make sure that the cooking dish for the aubergines is heatproof or ovenproof for steaming the aubergines.

Cook's Tip

Serve the pork garnished with a radish rose, turnip flowers and coriander leaves if liked.
   Should the skin still not be crisp enough at the end of the cooking time then place under a preheated hot grill for 1–2 minutes to crisp.

153 | Twice-Cooked Pork with Chilli Bean Sauce

Preparation time
15 minutes

Cooking time
about 35–40 minutes

Serves 3–4

Calories
550–400 per portion

You will need
350 g/12 oz belly pork in one
   piece, not too lean
100 g/4 oz bamboo shoots
100 g/4 oz celery sticks
3 tablespoons oil
2 spring onions, chopped
1 garlic clove, chopped
2 tablespoons sake or dry sherry
1 tablespoon soy sauce
1 tablespoon chilli bean paste

Place the whole piece of pork in a pan of boiling water and cook for 25–30 minutes. Remove and leave to cool.

Cut across the grain of the meat into thin slices, about 5×2.5 cm/2×1 inch in size. Cut the bamboo shoots and celery into chunks roughly the same size.

Heat the oil in a wok or deep frying pan until smoking, add the spring onions and garlic to flavour the oil, then add the vegetables and stir a few times. Add the pork, followed by the sake or sherry, soy and chilli bean sauces. Stir-fry for about 1–2 minutes. Serve hot.

154 | Grilled Ginger Pork

Preparation time
10 minutes, plus 30
minutes marinating
time

Cooking time
about 35 minutes

Serves 4

Calories
150 per portion

You will need
2 pork fillets, each weighing
   175–225 g/6–6 oz
5 cm/2 inch piece root ginger,
   grated
4 tablespoons soy sauce

Put the pork fillets in a shallow dish, add the ginger and soy sauce and leave to marinate for at least 30 minutes.

Wrap each fillet in foil, reserving the marinade. Place under a preheated hot grill for 5 minutes, then turn the grill down to low and cook for a further 20–25 minutes or until thoroughly cooked.

Unwrap the pork and cut each fillet into 1-cm/½-inch slices. Place on warmed individual plates. Pour the meat juices from the foil into a pan and add the reserved marinade. If there is not enough sauce add a few spoonfuls of water and soy sauce to taste. Bring to the boil and simmer for 5 minutes. Pour over the meat and serve at once.

Cook's Tip

To be authentic, the cut of meat usually used in this dish is belly of pork, known as 'five-flower' pork in China because the alternate layers of fat and meat form a pretty pink and white pattern when viewed in cross-section.

Cook's Tip

This is an easy, economical Japanese dish, which nonetheless is delicious enough to be served at dinner parties. Serve with French beans and plain boiled rice if wished. Garnish with grated daikon (Japanese radish).

155 | Braised Pork with Bamboo Shoots

Preparation time
20 minutes, including soaking time

Cooking time
about 25 minutes

Serves 4

Calories
500 per portion

You will need
2 tablespoons oil
3 slices root ginger, chopped
1 spring onion, chopped
675 g/1½ lb pork shoulder, cubed
2 tablespoons dry sherry
2 tablespoons soy sauce
1 (227-g/8-oz) can bamboo shoots, drained and chopped
4 medium dried Chinese mushrooms, soaked for 20 minutes, drained, stemmed and quartered
2 teaspoons garlic salt
1 teaspoon sugar
300 ml/½ pint water

Heat the oil in a pan, add the ginger and spring onion and stir-fry for 30 seconds. Add the pork and stir-fry for 2 minutes or until lightly browned. Add the sherry and soy sauce and stir for 1 minute, then add the bamboo shoots and mushrooms and stir-fry for 30 seconds. Add the garlic salt, sugar and water, bring to the boil, cover and simmer for 20 minutes. Serve hot.

156 | Pork with Mushrooms and Bamboo Shoots

Preparation time
25–30 minutes

Cooking time
about 5 minutes

Serves 4

Calories
220 per portion

You will need
4 dried Chinese mushrooms
225 g/8 oz pork fillet
2 tablespoons soy sauce
1 tablespoon cornflour
225 g/8 oz bamboo shoots
4 tablespoons oil
1½ teaspoons salt
2 tablespoons dry sherry

Soak the mushrooms in warm water for 20 minutes, drain, remove the stalks and halve or quarter the caps, depending upon size. Retain the soaking liquid.

Cut the pork into thin slices about the size of a postage stamp. Mix together the soy sauce and cornflour, then add the pork and toss to coat. Cut the bamboo shoots into thin slices the same size as the pork.

Heat about half of the oil in a wok or frying pan and stir-fry the pork slices for about 1 minute until lightly coloured. Remove with a slotted spoon and set aside.

Add the remaining oil and heat; add the mushrooms and bamboo shoots, then the salt, pork and sherry, stirring well. Cook for a further minute or so, stirring constantly and, if necessary, add a little of the reserved mushroom-soaking liquid. Serve hot.

Cook's Tip

This recipe comes from the Cantonese region of southern China and illustrates how this type of cooking does not depend so much on hot spicy ingredients as its neighbour Szechuan, but more on the subtle flavouring of soy sauce.

Mainly light soy sauce is used in recipes as opposed to the dark variety so that it does not detract from the colours of the other ingredients in a dish.

Cook's Tip

This quickly cooked and crisp-textured meat and vegetable dish is best served with a fried rice accompaniment.

157 | Pork Meatballs with Vegetables

Preparation time
20 minutes

Cooking time
about 35 minutes

Serves 4

Calories
350 per portion

You will need
450 g/1 lb minced pork
2 tablespoons soy sauce
1 tablespoon dry sherry
1¼ teaspoons sugar
1 egg, beaten
1 tablespoon cornflour
3 tablespoons oil
2 slices root ginger, shredded
2 spring onions, chopped
225 g/8 oz Chinese cabbage or
    greens, cut into small pieces
3–4 dried Chinese mushrooms,
    soaked for 20 minutes, drained,
    stems discarded and caps
    chopped
1 teaspoon salt
100 g/4 oz cellophane noodles
3 tablespoons stock or water

Mix the pork with the soy sauce, sherry, sugar, egg and cornflour. Divide and shape into 12 meatballs.

Heat the oil, add the meatballs and fry until golden. Remove with a slotted spoon and set aside. Add the ginger and spring onion to the pan, then the cabbage and mushrooms and fry for 1–2 minutes.

Add the salt, stir a few times, then add the meatballs and the noodles. Moisten with the stock or water and bring to the boil. Reduce the heat, cover and simmer for about 20–25 minutes. Serve hot.

158 | Thai Fried Pork Balls

Preparation time
20 minutes

Cooking time
about 12 minutes

Serves 4

Calories
320 per portion

You will need
2 coriander roots, finely chopped
2 teaspoons black pepper
4 garlic cloves
pinch of sugar
450 g/1 lb minced pork
2 tablespoons fish sauce
flour for coating
4–5 tablespoons oil
fresh coriander leaves to garnish

Put the coriander roots, pepper, garlic and sugar in a blender or food processor and work to a paste. Add the pork and mix well. Add the fish sauce, blending well, then divide and shape into 20 balls about 2.5 cm/1 inch in diameter. Dust in the flour.

Heat the oil and add about 5 meatballs and fry over a moderate heat for about 2–3 minutes, or until no liquid is released from the balls when pierced with a sharp knife. Remove from the pan and keep hot while frying the remainder in batches.

Pile into a warmed serving dish and garnish with fresh coriander leaves. Serve hot.

Cook's Tip

Chinese cabbage, also known as Pe-tsai, is a versatile vegetable used a great deal in Chinese cooking. Long in shape, and similar to the cos lettuce, it can be steamed, lightly cooked, stir-fried or eaten raw.

Cook's Tip

Serve this dish with a plain boiled rice. For the Thais, plain boiled rice is the basis of all meals. 'Plain' is the right description – they tend to salt the rice very lightly, since the other dishes are so highly seasoned, particularly with their favourite flavouring, nam pla or fish sauce.

159 | Casserole of Lion's Head

Preparation time
20 minutes

Cooking time
25–30 minutes

Serves 4–6

Calories
400–260 per portion

You will need
675 g/1½ lb finely minced pork
1 teaspoon salt
2 garlic cloves, crushed
2 (2.5-cm/1-inch) pieces root
    ginger, chopped
4 tablespoons soy sauce
3 tablespoons dry sherry
4 spring onions, chopped
1 tablespoon cornflour
oil for deep frying
300 ml/½ pint beef stock
675 g/1½ lb spinach
chopped spring onion to garnish

Mix the pork with the salt, garlic, ginger, 1 tablespoon each of the soy sauce and sherry and 2 of the spring onions. Mix in the cornflour, then divide and shape into balls the size of a walnut.

Heat the oil and deep-fry the pork balls until golden. Drain well, then place in a pan with the remaining soy sauce, sherry and spring onions. Spoon over the stock, cover and simmer for 15–20 minutes.

Meanwhile, cook the spinach with just the water clinging to the leaves after washing, for 5–10 minutes until tender. Transfer to a warmed serving dish, arrange the meatballs on top and garnish with spring onion and serve at once.

Cook's Tip

This recipe comes from eastern China. Eastern Chinese food is traditionally divided into a number of regional styles. Lion's head is a speciality of the Huai Yang school in the north of the region.

160 | Chilli Pork Spareribs

Preparation time
15 minutes

Cooking time
45 minutes

Serves 4–6

Calories
350–240 per portion

You will need
1 kg/2 lb lean pork spareribs
salt
2 tablespoons oil
2 dried red chillies
2.5 cm/1 inch piece root ginger,
    finely chopped
1 garlic clove, thinly sliced

For the sauce
4 tablespoons clear honey
4 tablespoons wine vinegar
2 tablespoons light soy sauce
2 tablespoons dry sherry
1 (142-g/5-oz) can tomato purée
1 teaspoon chilli powder
2 garlic cloves, crushed

Mix all the sauce ingredients together and set aside. Cut the spareribs into 5-cm/2-inch pieces and sprinkle over with salt.

Heat the oil and quickly fry the red chillies, then remove from the oil. Add the ginger and garlic and stir-fry for 30 seconds. Add the spareribs and fry for 5 minutes, until golden brown. Lower the heat and cook gently for 10 minutes.

Add the sauce to the pan, cover and simmer gently for 25–30 minutes. Serve hot.

Cook's Tip

If liked, the cooked hot spareribs can be garnished with a little chopped or shredded spring onion. Serve with a finger bowl and napkin.

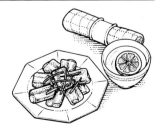

161 | *Pork Vindaloo*

Preparation time
10 minutes, plus
overnight standing time

Cooking time
about 50 minutes

Serves 4

Calories
370 per portion

You will need
1–2 teaspoons chilli powder
1 teaspoon turmeric
2 teaspoons ground cumin
2 teaspoons ground mustard
2 tablespoons ground coriander
2.5 cm/1 inch piece root ginger,
  chopped
salt
150 ml/¼ pint vinegar
1 large onion, finely chopped
2 garlic cloves, crushed
675 g/1½ lb pork fillet, cubed
4 tablespoons oil

Mix the spices and salt to taste with the vinegar. Put the onion, garlic and pork in a bowl, pour over the vinegar mixture, cover and leave in the refrigerator overnight.

Heat the oil in a large pan, add the pork mixture, bring to simmering point, cover and cook for about 45 minutes or until the pork is tender.

162 | *Aubergine and Pork in Hot Sauce*

Preparation time
about 25 minutes

Cooking time
about 10 minutes

Serves 4

Calories
230 per portion

You will need
175 g/6 oz boned lean pork,
  shredded
2 spring onions, chopped
1 slice root ginger, chopped
1 garlic clove, chopped
1 tablespoon soy sauce
2 teaspoons sake or sherry
1½ teaspoons cornflour
oil for deep frying
225 g/8 oz aubergine, cut into
  diamond-shaped chunks
1 tablespoon chilli sauce
3–4 tablespoons chicken stock or
  water
chopped spring onions to garnish

Put the pork in a bowl with the spring onions, ginger, garlic, soy sauce, sake or sherry and cornflour. Mix well and leave to stand for 20 minutes.

Heat the oil to 180 C/350 F and deep-fry the aubergine for about 1½ minutes. Remove with a slotted spoon and drain on absorbent kitchen paper.

Pour off all but 1 tablespoon oil from the pan, then add the pork mixture and stir-fry for about 1 minute. Add the aubergine and chilli sauce and cook for 1½ minutes, then moisten with stock or water. Simmer until the liquid has almost completely evaporated. Serve hot, garnished with chopped spring onions.

Cook's Tip

Vindaloo is a particular way of cooking. The amount of chillies or chilli powder used is not the most important aspect of this cooking style – the object is that you should be able to taste the nuances of flavour.

Cook's Tip

A quick way of scooping out and chopping aubergines is to cut them in half, then cut the middle criss-cross with a sharp knife. Carefully cut out the flesh or scoop out with a spoon.

163 | *Fried Pork with Baby Corn*

Preparation time
5 minutes

Cooking time
about 5 minutes

Serves 4

Calories
260 per portion

You will need
1 tablespoon dry sherry
1 tablespoon soy sauce
1½ teaspoons cornflour
450 g/1 lb pork fillet, sliced as
   thinly as possible
1 tablespoon oil
50 g/2 oz mangetout
1 teaspoon salt
1 (425-g/15-oz) can baby corn,
   drained
1 (425-g/15-oz) can straw
   mushrooms, drained
2 teaspoons sugar

Mix the sherry and soy sauce with 1 teaspoon of the corn-flour. Add the pork and toss to coat well. Heat the oil in a pan, add the pork and stir-fry until lightly browned. Add the mangetout and salt and stir-fry for 30 seconds. Add the baby corn and mushrooms and stir-fry for 1 minute. Sprinkle in the sugar.

Mix the remaining cornflour with 2 teaspoons water and stir into the pan. Cook, stirring continuously until thickened. Serve at once.

164 | *Stir-Fried Liver with Spinach*

Preparation time
10 minutes

Cooking time
about 3–4 minutes

Serves 4

Calories
300 per portion

You will need
350 g/12 oz pig's liver, cut into
   thin triangular slices
2 tablespoons cornflour
4 tablespoons oil
450 g/1 lb spinach leaves, rinsed
1 teaspoon salt
2 thin slices root ginger
1 tablespoon soy sauce
1 tablespoon rice wine or sherry
   (see Cook's Tip)
shredded spring onion to garnish

Blanch the liver for a few seconds in boiling water, then drain and coat with cornflour.

Heat 2 tablespoons of the oil in a wok or frying pan. Add the spinach and salt and stir-fry for 2 minutes. Remove from the pan and arrange around the edge of a warmed serving dish. Keep hot.

Heat the remaining oil in a pan until it is very hot. Add the ginger, liver, soy sauce and wine or sherry. Stir well, then pour over the spinach. Avoid overcooking the liver or it will become tough. Stir well and pour over the spinach.

Serve at once, garnished with chopped spring onions.

Cook's Tip

This is a recipe from the Canton region of southern China. This dish illustrates the quick stir-fry method of cooking that is so typical of Cantonese cooking – a way of cooking that helps to retain nutrients, colour and flavour of foods. It is a colourful and aromatic way to cook food which has done much to spread the popularity of Chinese cooking all over the world.

Cook's Tip

The two most popular wines in China are the white and yellow wines made from rice. The ordinary yellow rice wine called shaosing is used for cooking.

Poultry Dishes

Many of the Orient's classic recipes feature poultry in all its guises and have become world wide favourites. These include the classic Peking duck, chop suey, Pleasure-boat duck, Nanking spiced duck and Tandoori chicken. Try them alongside some Chinese newcomers like chicken in sesame sauce, braised chicken wings and turkey parcels; or ring the changes and choose a less-known Indian dish like Butter Chicken or Yogurt Chicken.

165 | Stir-Fried Lemony Chicken

(Illustrated on back jacket)

Preparation time
20 minutes, including marinating time

Cooking time
4 minutes

Serves 4

Calories
200 per portion

You will need
350 g/12 oz boneless chicken
2 tablespoons dry sherry
4 spring onions, chopped
2.5 cm/1 inch piece root ginger, finely chopped
2 tablespoons oil
1–2 garlic cloves, sliced
2 celery sticks, sliced diagonally
1 small green pepper, cored, seeded and sliced
2 tablespoons light soy sauce
juice of ½ lemon
shredded rind of 2 lemons
¼ teaspoon chilli powder

Skin the chicken and cut into 7.5-cm/3-inch strips. Mix the sherry with the spring onions and ginger. Add the chicken and toss well to coat, then set aside for 15 minutes.

Heat the oil in a wok or frying pan, add the garlic, celery and green pepper and stir-fry for 1 minute. Add the chicken and marinade and cook for 2 minutes. Stir in the soy sauce, lemon juice and rind and chilli powder and cook for a further 1 minute.

Serve at once garnished as shown if liked.

166 | Kashmiri Chicken

Preparation time
10 minutes

Cooking time
about 40 minutes

Serves 6

Calories
320 per portion

You will need
100 g/4 oz butter
3 large onions, finely sliced
10 peppercorns
10 cardamoms
5 cm/2 inch piece cinnamon stick
5 cm/2 inch piece root ginger, chopped
2 cloves garlic, finely chopped
1 teaspoon chilli powder
2 teaspoons paprika
salt
1.5 kg/3 lb chicken pieces, skinned
250 g/8 oz natural yogurt

For the garnish
lime wedges
sprigs of parsley

Melt the butter in a deep, lidded frying pan or wok. Add the onions, peppercorns, cardamoms and cinnamon and fry until the onions are golden. Add the ginger, garlic, chilli powder, paprika and salt to taste and fry for 2 minutes, stirring occasionally.

Add the chicken pieces and fry until browned. Gradually add the yogurt, stirring constantly. Cover and cook for about 30 minutes. Serve hot, garnished with lime wedges and sprigs of parsley if liked.

Cook's Tip

When grating oranges or lemons, work on a sheet of greaseproof paper, using a pastry brush to remove all the rind from the grater. It is then a simple matter to brush the rind from the paper into the pan.

Cook's Tip

Yogurt is eaten daily all over India, either plain or with vegetables or fruit mixed in. It is also used in cooking, particularly in the north. There is a variety of yogurts to choose from in western stores: ordinary yogurt, semi set or the thick Greek-style yogurt. Select according to how thick you like your sauces.

167 | *Chicken in Sesame Sauce*

Preparation time
15 minutes, plus 30 minutes marinating time

Cooking time
3–5 minutes

Serves 4–6

Calories
500–340 per portion

You will need
450 g/1 lb boneless chicken breasts, cut into cubes
1 tablespoon oil
100 g/4 oz unsalted cashew nuts
75 g/3 oz canned straw mushrooms, drained and halved

For the marinade
3 spring onions, chopped
3 tablespoons soy sauce
2 tablespoons hot pepper oil
2 tablespoons sesame oil
1 tablespoon sesame seed paste or tahini
1 teaspoon ground Szechuan peppercorns

Put the marinade ingredients into a bowl. Add the chicken cubes, turning to coat thoroughly. Leave to marinate for 30 minutes.

Meanwhile, heat the oil in a wok or frying pan, add the cashew nuts and fry until golden. Drain on absorbent kitchen paper.

Add the chicken and marinade to the pan and stir-fry for 2 minutes. Add the mushrooms and cook for a further 1 minute. Pile the mixture into a warmed serving dish and sprinkle with the nuts. Serve at once.

Cook's Tip

Szechuan peppercorns are reddish-brown Chinese peppercorns with a specially pungent flavour. They are usually dry roasted in a frying pan before cooking to develop the full flavour.

168 | *Rice Cooked with Chicken*

Preparation time
30 minutes

Cooking time
about 3–3¼ hours

Serves 6

Calories
880 per portion

You will need
4 small onions, halved
2 bay leaves
1 litre/1¾ pints water
1.75 kg/4 lb boiling chicken
½ teaspoon saffron threads
675 g/1½ lb Basmati rice
100 g/4 oz ghee
5 garlic cloves, sliced
10 cloves
10 cardamoms
2 (7.5-cm/3-inch) cinnamon sticks
50 g/2 oz blanched almonds
100 g/4 oz sultanas

For the garnish
hard-boiled egg quarters
fried onion rings

Place the onion halves, bay leaves, 1 litre/1¾ pints water in a pan and bring to the boil. Add the chicken, cover and simmer for 1½–2 hours until tender. Remove the flesh from the chicken and cut into pieces; reserve the cooking liquid and onions. Put the saffron in a cup and pour over a little boiling water; leave for 20 minutes. Wash the rice well.

Heat the ghee in a pan, add the reserved onions, garlic, cloves, cardamoms and cinnamon and fry for 5 minutes. Add the rice and enough cooking liquid to cover the rice, then the strained saffron water. Cook, uncovered, for 10–15 minutes, then cover to cook until tender. Mix with the chicken, almonds and sultanas. Garnish and serve.

Cook's Tip

To prevent black rings forming around the yolks of hard-boiled eggs, after cooking drain and leave in a saucepan under a running cold tap for about 2 minutes.

169 | Soy-Braised Chicken

Preparation time
10 minutes, plus 10–15 minutes marinating time

Cooking time
about 50 minutes

Serves 4

Calories
500 per portion

You will need
1.5 kg/3½ lb young chicken
1 teaspoon salt
1 tablespoon sugar
3 tablespoons light soy sauce
2 tablespoons dark soy sauce
3 tablespoons sake or dry sherry
1 tablespoon cornflour
3 tablespoons vegetable oil
2 slices root ginger, peeled
2–3 spring onions, chopped
1 garlic clove, crushed
300 ml/½ pint clear stock or water
450 g/1 lb carrots, peeled
225 g/8 oz mushrooms, wiped
fresh coriander leaves to garnish

Joint the chicken and cut into about 20–24 pieces, leaving the skin on. Place in a bowl with the salt, sugar, soy sauces, sake and cornflour. Mix well, cover and marinate for 10–15 minutes.

Heat the oil, add the ginger, spring onions and garlic, add the strained chicken pieces and stir-fry for 5 minutes until lightly browned. Add the marinade with the stock or water, bring to the boil, reduce the heat, cover and simmer for 25–30 minutes.

Slice the carrots and mushrooms and add to the chicken. Increase the heat and cook for a further 10–15 minutes until most of the liquid has evaporated. Serve hot, garnished with coriander leaves.

Cook's Tip

Soy-braised or red-cooked chicken is one of the most popular ways of preparing poultry in China. If preferred, use an assortment of different chicken pieces instead of the whole chicken suggested in this recipe.

170 | Chicken in Coconut Milk

Preparation time
30 minutes

Cooking time
about 40 minutes

Serves 4

Calories
290 per portion

You will need
1.5 kg/3½ lb chicken, cut into 8 pieces
900 ml/1½ pints coconut milk (see Cook's Tip recipe 3)
5 cm/2 inch piece lengkuas (see Cook's Tip)
3 green chillies, seeded
8 stems coriander
4 citrus leaves (optional)
a few black peppercorns, crushed
1 teaspoon grated lime rind
salt
2 tablespoons fish sauce
1 tablespoon lime juice
fresh coriander leaves to garnish

Skin the chicken and place in a pan. Skim off the coconut cream from the milk and reserve. Pour the remaining milk over the chicken. Finely chop the lengkuas, chillies and coriander. Add to the pan the citrus leaves, if using, the crushed peppercorns, lime rind and salt to taste. Bring to the boil, reduce the heat and simmer, uncovered, for 35–40 minutes or until the chicken is tender and half of the liquid has evaporated.

About 5 minutes before serving, pour in the reserved coconut cream and bring to the boil. Add the fish sauce and lime juice. Transfer to a warmed serving dish and sprinkle with coriander leaves to garnish.

Cook's Tip

Lengkuas is a delicately pine-flavoured root. It is also available dried as laos powder. If using laos powder instead of the fresh root then use 1 teaspoon laos powder for each 1-cm/½-inch piece of root specified in the recipe.

171 | Chicken with Shrimp Sauce

Preparation time
30 minutes

Cooking time
about 40 minutes

Serves 4

Calories
440 per portion

You will need
1.5 kg/3½ lb chicken joints
1 onion, quartered
4 garlic cloves, peeled
2.5 cm/1 inch piece root ginger, peeled and chopped
3 red chillies, seeded and quartered
1 tablespoon water
3 tablespoons vegetable oil
1 teaspoon turmeric
1 teaspoon pepper
½ teaspoon dried shrimp paste (see Cook's Tip recipe 239)
½ teaspoon laos powder (see Cook's Tip recipe 170)
2 strips lemon rind
2 teaspoons patis (see Cook's Tip)
1½ teaspoons salt
30 ml/½ pint coconut milk
1 tablespoon sugar
2 tablespoons lemon juice

Cut the chicken into 4-cm/1½-inch pieces. Purée the onion, garlic, ginger and chillies with the water.

Heat the oil, fry the onion mixture for 3–4 minutes then add the turmeric, pepper, shrimp paste and laos and cook for 1 minute. Add the lemon rind, patis, salt and chicken pieces and stir-fry until beginning to brown. Add the coconut milk and sugar and simmer, cover and cook for 30 minutes until tender.

Stir in the lemon juice and serve at once.

Cook's Tip

Patis is a shrimp or fish sauce, rather similar to nam pla. It is available from Oriental stores.

172 | Lemon Chicken

Preparation time
25 minutes

Cooking time
about 5 minutes

Serves 4

Calories
550 per portion

You will need
1.5 kg/3½ lb chicken, boned and cubed
salt and pepper
5 tablespoons oil
15 g/½ oz lard
4 slices root ginger, chopped
1 red pepper, seeded and sliced
5–6 dried Chinese mushrooms, soaked for 20 minutes and shredded
shredded rind of 2 lemons
5 spring onions, sliced
4 tablespoons dry sherry
1½ teaspoons sugar
2 tablespoons soy sauce
1 teaspoon cornflour
1–2 tablespoons lemon juice

Rub the chicken with 1½ teaspoons salt, pepper to taste and 1½ tablespoons of the oil. Heat the remaining oil in a pan until hot. Add the chicken and stir-fry for 2 minutes, remove and keep warm.

Add the lard to the pan and melt. Add the ginger, pepper and squeezed and shredded mushrooms and stir-fry for 1 minute. Add the lemon rind and spring onions. Stir-fry for 30 seconds. Sprinkle in the sherry, sugar and soy sauce. Add the cornflour dissolved in 1 tablespoon water and stir for 1 minute. Sprinkle in the lemon juice and serve at once.

Cook's Tip

Red peppers (which are simply ripe green peppers) are a good source of vitamins A and C. Look for plump, firm pods with bright colour. To deseed, slice off the top, then cut around the pith to remove the core and seeds cleanly.

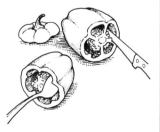

173 | *Butter Chicken*

Preparation time
30 minutes, plus 4–5
hours marinating time

Cooking time
50–60 minutes

Oven temperature
220 C, 425 F, gas 7

Serves 8

Calories
370 per portion

You will need
1.5 kg/3½ lb chicken, cut into 8
    pieces
salt
1 tablespoon lemon juice
1 green chilli, chopped
7 g/¼ oz root ginger, peeled
3 small garlic cloves, peeled
150 ml/¼ pint natural yogurt
2 teaspoons paprika
¼ teaspoon chilli powder
orange food colouring (optional)
a little melted butter
175 g/6 oz unsalted butter
150 ml/¼ pint soured cream

Make sharp slits through the skin of the chicken, rub with salt and sprinkle with lemon juice. Purée the chilli with the ginger and garlic. Mix with the yogurt, paprika, chilli powder and orange colouring if liked. Mix with the chicken and marinate for 4–5 hours.

Remove the chicken portions and place on a baking tray and bake for 45–50 minutes, brushing with a little butter occasionally.

Melt the butter in a pan, add the marinade and soured cream and heat, without boiling for 5–6 minutes. Pour over the chicken to serve.

174 | *Chicken Vindaloo*

Preparation time
20 minutes

Cooking time
about 1 hour

Serves 4

Calories
800 per portion

You will need
1.5 kg/3½ lb chicken
2 large onions, chopped
225 g/8 oz ghee
2 green chillies
25 g/1 oz root ginger, chopped
3 garlic cloves, chopped
1½ teaspoons turmeric
1 teaspoon ground coriander
1 teaspoon garam masala (see
    Cook's Tip recipe 67)
2 tablespoons vinegar
2 curry leaves (optional)
300 ml/½ pint water
1 teaspoon salt
50 g/2 oz desiccated coconut
chopped fresh coriander to
    garnish

Skin and joint the chicken. Fry the onions in the ghee with the green chillies until golden. Add the ginger, garlic, turmeric, coriander and garam masala. Fry for a further 3 minutes.

Add the vinegar, curry leaves, if used, water and chicken. Cover and simmer for 30 minutes. Test to check that the chicken is cooked (see Cook's Tip), remove the lid and boil rapidly until the liquid evaporates.

Add the salt and coconut and simmer for 15 minutes. Serve sprinkled with chopped coriander.

Cook's Tip

**50 g/2 oz finely chopped
cashew nuts or almonds can
be added to the simmering
sauce if liked. Serve as a main
course with Naan bread (see
recipe 219).**

Cook's Tip

**The chicken is cooked when
the juices run clear after being
pierced in the thickest part of
the flesh or thigh with a knife
or skewer.**

175 | *Yogurt Chicken*

Preparation time
10 minutes, plus 8
hours marinating time

Cooking time
about 1¼–1½ hours

Oven temperature
200 C, 400 F, gas 6
then
180 C, 350 F, gas 4

Serves 4

Calories
280 per portion

You will need
1.5 kg/3½ lb chicken, skinned
2 tablespoons lemon juice
1 teaspoon salt
250 ml/8 fl oz natural yogurt
½ bunch fresh coriander leaves,
    finely chopped
5 cm/2 inch piece root ginger,
    peeled and chopped
4 garlic cloves, finely chopped
2 small green chillies, seeded and
    finely chopped

For the garnish (optional)
cucumber slices
lemon slices

Prick the chicken all over and rub with the lemon juce and salt. Cover and leave to stand for 30 minutes.

Mix the yogurt with the coriander, ginger, garlic and chillies, rub over the chicken and leave to stand for 7–8 hours.

Place in a roasting tin and cook at the higher temperature for 30 minutes. Reduce the temperature and cook for a further 45 minutes or until cooked. Remove the chicken from the juices and keep warm. Skim off the fat from the juices, bring to the boil and cook for 2–3 minutes until thickened. Pour over the chicken and garnish with cucumber and lemon slices if liked.

176 | *Chilli Chicken*

Preparation time
15 minutes

Cooking time
about 10 minutes

Serves 4

Calories
360 per portion

You will need
675 g/1½ lb boneless chicken
    breasts, cubed
1 teaspoon sugar
3–6 red chillies
4 almonds
1 stem lemon grass, sliced
1 teaspoon fenugreek
2.5 cm/1 inch slice root ginger,
    peeled
6 small red onions or shallots,
    peeled and sliced
4 garlic cloves, crushed
4 tablespoons oil
150 ml/¼ pint water
salt
shredded spring onion to garnish

Sprinkle the chicken with the sugar. Purée the chillies with the nuts, lemon grass, fenugreek and half the ginger. Purée the remaining ginger with the onions and the garlic.

Heat the oil and fry the spice mixture for 1–2 minutes. Add the onion mixture and fry for 1–2 minutes. Add the chicken pieces and stir to coat. Add the water and salt to taste. Cover and cook gently for 5 minutes.

Transfer to a serving dish and sprinkle with the shredded spring onion to serve.

Cook's Tip

To test whether a chicken is cooked, push a skewer into the meaty part. If any red juices flow out, the chicken is not yet cooked.

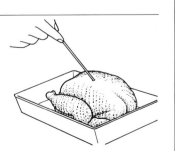

Cook's Tip

Fresh red hot chillies are a major and important ingredient in this recipe both for their flavour and colour. They may be seeded if liked before use.

177 | Ginger Chicken

Preparation time
10 minutes, plus 20–30
minutes standing time

Cooking time
about 10 minutes

Serves 4

Calories
370 per portion

You will need
675 g/1½ lb chicken breasts, cut
    into finger-sized pieces
1 teaspoon sugar
salt and pepper
4 tablespoons sesame oil
10 cm/4 inch piece root ginger,
    peeled and finely sliced
75–100 ml/3–4 fl oz water
100 g/4 oz button mushrooms
2 tablespoons brandy
2 teaspoons cornflour, blended
    with 3 tablespoons water
1 teaspoon soy sauce

Sprinkle the chicken with the sugar and leave to stand for 20–30 minutes. Season with salt and pepper.

Heat the oil and fry the ginger for 1 minute. Add the chicken pieces and cook for 3 minutes. Stir in the water and mushrooms. Cover and cook for a further 5 minutes, or until the chicken is tender.

Add the brandy, cornflour mixture and soy sauce. Bring to the boil, stirring, until thickened. Serve at once.

178 | Braised Chicken Wings

Preparation time
15 minutes

Cooking time
about 10 minutes

Serves 4

Calories
400 per portion

You will need
12 chicken wings
4 dried Chinese mushrooms,
    soaked in warm water for
    20–30 minutes
2 tablespoons oil
2 spring onions, finely chopped
2 slices root ginger, chopped
2 tablespoons soy sauce
2 tablespoons sake or sherry
1 tablespoon sugar
½ teaspoon 5-spice powder
350 ml/12 fl oz water
175 g/6 oz bamboo shoots, cubed
2 teaspoons cornflour, mixed with
    1 tablespoon water

Remove and discard the tips of the chicken wings, then cut each wing into 2 pieces by breaking the joint.

Squeeze the mushrooms dry, discard the stalks and slice the caps.

Heat the oil until smoking, add the spring onions and ginger, then the chicken wings. Stir-fry until the chicken changes colour, then add the soy sauce, sake, sugar, 5-spice powder and water. Lower the heat and cook until the liquid is reduced by about half. Add the mushrooms and bamboo shoots and continue to cook until nearly all the juices have evaporated. Remove the bamboo chunks, wash and place around a serving dish.

Add the cornflour to the chicken and stir until any juices are thickened. Place in a serving dish and serve at once.

Cook's Tip

Never dip mushrooms into water when cleaning them; they will absorb too much water and will be difficult to fry. Just wipe them over with a damp cloth.

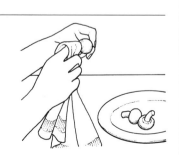

Cook's Tip

Chinese 5-spice powder is an aromatic seasoning made from a selection of 5 ground spices: star anise, fennel, cloves, cinnamon and szechuan pepper. It is used sparingly since it has an intense flavour.

179 | Diced Chicken with Chillies

Preparation time
10 minutes

Cooking time
4 minutes

Serves 4

Calories
200 per portion

You will need
2 tablespoons oil
1 garlic clove, sliced
350 g/12 oz boneless chicken breast, diced
1 red pepper, cored, seeded and diced
2 green chillies, seeded and sliced
50 g/2 oz beansprouts
2 tablespoons soy sauce
2 tablespoons chilli sauce
fresh coriander leaves to garnish

Heat the oil in a wok or frying pan, add the garlic and fry for 1 minute. Add the chicken and stir-fry for 1 minute. Add the pepper and chillies and cook for a further 1 minute. Stir in the beansprouts, soy sauce and chilli sauce and cook for 2 minutes.

Turn into a warm serving dish, garnish with coriander and serve at once.

180 | Stir-Fried Chicken with Ginger

Preparation time
10 minutes

Cooking time
12–15 minutes

Serves 4

Calories
300 per portion

You will need
2.5 cm/1 inch piece root ginger, peeled and shredded
salt
2 tablespoons oil
2 garlic cloves, chopped
6 chicken thighs, chopped into 2.5-cm/1-inch squares
1 tablespoon fish sauce
1 teaspoon sugar
1 tablespoon water
2 spring onions, cut into 5-cm/2-inch pieces
parsley sprigs to garnish

Sprinkle the ginger with salt, leave to stand a few minutes then squeeze and discard the liquid. Rinse and squeeze out again.

Heat the oil, add the garlic and stir-fry for 1–2 minutes. Add the ginger and stir-fry for 1 minute. Add the chicken and remaining ingredients, except the spring onions and parsley, then cover and cook over a moderate heat for 10 minutes, or until the chicken is cooked.

Stir in the spring onions and serve at once, garnished with parsley sprigs.

Cook's Tip

Chilli sauce is a very hot sauce made from chillies, vinegar and salt. Tabasco sauce can be used as a substitute.

Cook's Tip

Fresh root ginger may be stored in a plastic bag in the refrigerator for several weeks, but check to make sure that any cut ends do not develop a mould.

181 | *Chicken with Sesame Seeds*

Preparation time
20 minutes, including
marinating time

Cooking time
4 minutes

Serves 4

Calories
230 per portion

You will need
350 g/12 oz boneless chicken
1 egg white
½ teaspoon salt
2 teaspoons cornflour
2 tablespoons white sesame
    seeds
2 tablespoons oil
1 tablespoon dark soy sauce
1 tablespoon wine vinegar
½ teaspoon chilli bean sauce
½ teaspoon sesame oil
1 tablespoon dry sherry
½ teaspoon roasted Szechuan
    peppercorns
4 spring onions, chopped

Cut the chicken into 7.5-cm/3-inch long shreds. Mix the egg white, salt and cornflour, toss in the chicken and mix well. Leave to stand for 15 minutes.

Fry the sesame seeds until golden in a pan or wok. Remove and set aside.

Heat the oil, add the chicken and stir-fry for 1 minute. Remove with a slotted spoon. Add the soy sauce, vinegar, chilli bean sauce, sesame oil, sherry and peppercorns and bring to the boil. Add the chicken and spring onions and cook for 2 minutes. Sprinkle with the sesame seeds and serve at once.

182 | *Chicken Curry*

Preparation time
15 minutes, plus 4
hours marinating time

Cooking time
about 35 minutes

Serves 4

Calories
350 per portion

You will need
2 garlic cloves, chopped
5 cm/2 inch piece root ginger,
    peeled and chopped
1 teaspoon turmeric
2 teaspoons cumin seeds, ground
1 teaspoon chilli powder
1 teaspoon pepper
3 tablespoons finely chopped
    fresh coriander leaves
450 g/1 lb natural yogurt
salt
1 kg/2 lb chicken pieces, skinned
4 tablespoons oil
2 onions, chopped

Put the garlic, ginger, turmeric, cumin, chilli, pepper, coriander, yogurt and salt to taste into a large bowl. Mix well, add the chicken and leave for 4 hours, turning the chicken occasionally.

Heat the oil in a pan, add the onions and fry until golden. Add the chicken and the marinade. Bring to simmering point, cover and cook for about 30 minutes, until the chicken is tender.

Cook's Tip

You can 'chop' spring onions very simply by first washing them, then holding them over a bowl. Snip them up from the green end towards the root with a pair of scissors.

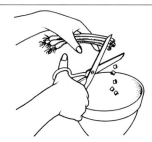

Cook's Tip

It is difficult to grind just a teaspoon or two of spices in a blender or food processor – this is best done in a pestle and mortar, coffee grinder or small herb mill.

183 | *Spicy Chicken and Peanuts*

Preparation time
5 minutes

Cooking time
3½ minutes

Serves 4

Calories
380 per portion

You will need
100 g/4 oz unsalted peanuts
350 g/12 oz boneless chicken
2 tablespoons oil
1 dried red chilli
2 tablespoons dry sherry
1 tablespoon dark soy sauce
pinch of sugar
1 garlic clove, crushed
2 spring onions, chopped
2.5 cm/1 inch piece root ginger,
   peeled and finely chopped
1 teaspoon wine vinegar
2 teaspoons sesame oil

Immerse the peanuts in boiling water for about 2 minutes. Drain and remove the skins, then dry well. Skin and cut the chicken into cubes.

  Heat the oil, crumble in the chilli, add the chicken and peanuts and stir-fry for 1 minute; remove from the pan. Add the sherry, soy sauce, sugar, garlic, spring onions, ginger and vinegar, bring to the boil then simmer for 30 seconds. Return the chicken, chilli and peanuts to the pan and cook for 2 minutes. Sprinkle over the sesame oil. Serve at once while very hot.

184 | *Chicken in Foil*

Preparation time
15 minutes, plus 15–20
minutes marinating
time

Cooking time
10–12 minutes

Serves 4–6

Calories
190–125 per portion

You will need
1 tablespoon soy sauce
1 tablespoon dry sherry
1 tablespoon sesame oil
450 g/1 lb boneless chicken
  breast, cut into 16 pieces
4 spring onions, each cut into 4
  pieces
2 pieces root ginger, shredded
1 celery stick, shredded

Mix the soy sauce, sherry and sesame oil together. Add the chicken and toss well to coat, then leave to marinate for 15–20 minutes.

  Cut out 16 pieces foil large enough to enclose the pieces of chicken generously. Brush the foil with oil, place a piece of chicken in the centre and top with a piece of spring onion, some ginger and celery. Fold over the foil to enclose the chicken and seal the edges well. Place in a steamer and steam for 10–12 minutes. Serve hot.

Cook's Tip

This recipe is a classic western Chinese dish, better known as Gongbao Chicken. It looks good garnished with a chilli flower. To make a chilli flower – shred the chilli lengthways leaving 1 cm / ½ inch attached at the stem end. Place in iced water for about 1 hour to open.

Cook's Tip

The chicken should be served still in its foil jacket and diners should open their own packets to eat.

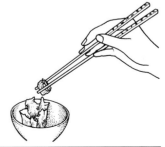

185 | *Cashew Chicken*

Preparation time
5 minutes

Cooking time
3 minutes

Serves 4

Calories
420 per portion

You will need
350 g/12 oz boneless chicken
1 egg white
4 tablespoons dry sherry
2 teaspoons cornflour
3 tablespoons oil
4 spring onions, chopped
2 garlic cloves, chopped
2.5 cm/1 inch piece root ginger,
    peeled and finely chopped
1 tablespoon light soy sauce
100 g/4 oz unsalted cashew nuts

Cut the chicken into 1-cm/½-inch cubes. Mix the egg white, half the sherry and the cornflour together, add the chicken and toss until evenly coated.

Heat the oil, add the spring onions, garlic and ginger and stir-fry for 30 seconds. Add the chicken and cook for 2 minutes. Pour in the remaining sherry and the soy sauce and stir well. Add the cashew nuts and cook for a further 30 seconds. Serve at once.

186 | *Chicken and Leeks*

Preparation time
25 minutes

Cooking time
2½ minutes

Serves 4

Calories
190 per portion

You will need
½ cucumber
salt
350 g/12 oz boneless chicken
    breasts, skinned
2 tablespoons oil
3 leeks, thinly sliced diagonally
4 garlic cloves, sliced
1 tablespoon light soy sauce
1 tablespoon dry sherry
1 dried red chilli, crumbled
1 tablespoon chopped fresh
    coriander leaves
coriander leaves to garnish

Peel the cucumber, cut in half and remove the seeds. Cut into 2.5-cm/1-inch cubes, place in a colander, sprinkle with salt and leave for 20 minutes. Cube the chicken.

Heat the oil, add the leeks and garlic and cook for 30 seconds. Add the chicken and brown for 1 minute. Add the soy sauce, sherry and chilli and cook for a further 30 seconds. Stir in the cucumber and cook for 30 seconds.

Serve hot sprinkled with chopped coriander and garnished with coriander leaves.

Cook's Tip

This chicken recipe originates from the southern region of China, and exemplifies the Chinese taste for contrasting textures. It also uses some of the best Chinese cooking principles: stir-frying to keep in the juices of the chicken, then stir-frying again with other ingredients to flavour it.

Cook's Tip

When cutting the chicken for this dish, and for most stir-fried dishes, always cut across the grain; this ensures tenderness and succulence after cooking.

187 | Deep-Fried Drumsticks

Preparation time
40 minutes, including marinating time

Cooking time
12–15 minutes

Serves 4

Calories
380 per portion

You will need
2 tablespoons dry sherry
2 tablespoons soy sauce
pinch of sugar
4 garlic cloves, crushed
2 teaspoons finely chopped root ginger
4 spring onions, chopped
8 chicken drumsticks
50 g/2 oz plain flour
1–2 eggs, beaten
oil for deep frying
lemon slices and parsley sprigs to garnish

Place the sherry, soy sauce, sugar, garlic, ginger and spring onions in a bowl. Add the chicken, turn to coat and leave for 30 minutes. Remove the chicken but reserve the marinade.

Sift the flour into a bowl and beat in the egg. Gradually beat in the marinade to form a smooth paste. Dip the chicken into the paste and turn to coat evenly. Heat the oil and deep-fry the chicken for 12–15 minutes until golden and cooked through. Drain and serve garnished with lemon slices and parsley sprigs.

188 | Green Chicken Curry

Preparation time
10 minutes

Cooking time
45 minutes

Serves 4

Calories
540 per portion

You will need
5 cm/2 inch piece root ginger, peeled and chopped
40 g/1½ oz fresh coriander leaves, chopped
2–4 green chillies, chopped
4 garlic cloves
2 onions, quartered
1 tablespoon plain flour
salt
1 teaspoon chilli powder
8 chicken thighs, skinned
3 tablespoons oil
300 ml/½ pint water
50 g/2 oz creamed coconut
juice of 1 lemon
lemon twists to garnish

Place the ginger, coriander, chillies, garlic and onions in a liquidizer or food processor and purée.

Mix the flour, 1 teaspoon salt and the chilli powder together and use to coat the chicken. Heat the oil, add the chicken and fry until golden. Remove and set aside.

Add the spice paste to the pan and fry, stirring for 5 minutes. Stir in the water and salt to taste, then return the chicken to the pan. Cover and simmer for 25 minutes.

Stir in the coconut, then add the lemon juice; cover and simmer for 10 minutes. Serve at once garnished with lemon twists.

Cook's Tip

It is important to get the fat or oil hot for deep frying. Use a fat thermometer or test by dropping a piece of fresh bread into the oil. If it turns golden and floats to the surface for a few seconds the oil is hot enough.

Cook's Tip

This green chicken curry gets its colour and flavour from coriander leaves. It goes well with rice and peas, or with Paratha (see recipe 222) or crusty French bread.

189 | Pineapple Chicken Curry

Preparation time
1 hour, including soaking time

Cooking time
45 minutes

Serves 4

Calories
620 per portion

You will need
2 onions, quartered
2 garlic cloves, peeled
3.5 cm/1½ inch piece root ginger, peeled and chopped
1 teaspoon turmeric
1 tablespoon ground coriander
1–2 teaspoons chilli powder
2 tablespoons paprika
1 teaspoon sugar
1 teaspoon salt
2 tablespoons oil
8 chicken thighs, skinned
300 ml/½ pint water
100 g/4 oz cashew nuts, soaked in boiling water for 1 hour
6 curry leaves
4 green chillies, slit
1 medium pineapple, cubed
juice of ½–1 lemon

Place the first 9 ingredients in a liquidizer or food processor and work until smooth.

Heat the oil, add the spice paste and fry for 10 minutes. Add the chicken pieces and fry for 5 minutes. Pour in the water and bring to simmering point. Add the drained nuts, curry leaves and chillies, cover and simmer for 25 minutes. Add the pineapple and lemon juice to taste and simmer for a further 10 minutes. Serve hot.

190 | Indonesian Spicy Chicken

Preparation time
35 minutes, including marinating time

Cooking time
45 minutes

Serves 4

Calories
400 per portion

You will need
8 chicken pieces, skinned
juice of 1 lemon
4 tablespoons desiccated coconut, soaked in 4 tablespoons hot water
2–4 red chillies, chopped
4 small onions, quartered
2 garlic cloves, peeled
4 Brazil nuts, shelled
1 cm/½ inch piece root ginger, peeled
1 teaspoon grated lemon rind
1 teaspoon shrimp paste
1 teaspoon sugar
1 teaspoon salt
3 tablespoons oil
300 ml/½ pint water

Rub the chicken pieces with the lemon juice and leave to stand for 20 minutes.

Put all the remaining ingredients except the oil and water in a liquidizer or food processor and work to a smooth paste. Heat the oil in a large pan and fry the paste, stirring, for 5 minutes.

Add the chicken and fry for 5 minutes. Stir in the water and cook, uncovered, for 30 minutes or until the chicken is tender and the sauce is thick. Serve hot.

Cook's Tip

Pineapple is the ideal fruit for a curry, combining acidity with sweetness and, when fresh, crispness. Canned pineapple chunks may be used, but they tend to be too sweet and bland.

Cook's Tip

Serve Indonesian Spicy Chicken with krupuk or prawn crisps, fried bananas and a selection of sambals.

191 | *Curried Chicken*

Preparation time
10 minutes

Cooking time
8 minutes

Serves 4

Calories
200 per portion

You will need
2 tablespoons oil
½ teaspoon cumin seeds
½ teaspoon ground cinnamon
seeds from 2 cardamoms,
  crushed
pepper
2 onions, chopped
1 heaped teaspoon chopped root
  ginger
2 garlic cloves, crushed
3–4 chicken breasts, skinned and
  cut into slivers
1 (400-g/14-oz) can tomatoes
1 tablespoon soy sauce
1–2 teaspoons sugar
½ teaspoon garam masala (see
  Cook's Tip recipe 67)

Heat the oil and fry the cumin seeds, cinnamon and cardamom seeds for 1 minute. Add the pepper, onions, ginger and garlic and fry for 2 minutes. Add the chicken pieces and stir-fry for about 5 minutes, until lightly coloured. Add the tomatoes, with their juice, soy sauce and sugar to taste. Bring to the boil, lower the heat and stir in the garam masala.

Serve at once.

192 | *Chicken with Lemon Sauce*

Preparation time
6 minutes

Cooking time
8 minutes

Serves 4

Calories
150 per portion

You will need
1 tablespoon oil
1 onion, finely chopped
1 garlic clove, crushed
2–3 chicken breasts, skinned and
  cut into thin slices
1 tablespoon soy sauce
50 g/2 oz small button
  mushrooms, sliced
finely grated rind of 1 lemon
4 tablespoons water
2 tablespoons single cream
pepper
watercress sprigs to garnish

Heat the oil, add the onion and cook, stirring, for 2 minutes. Stir in the garlic and push to one side of the pan. Tilt the pan to let the juices run out over the base. Add the chicken and stir-fry for 2 minutes over a high heat. Lower the heat, add the soy sauce and mushrooms and stir-fry for 1 minute, stirring in the already cooked garlic and onions. Stir in the lemon rind and water, then add the cream and heat through gently without boiling.

Season with pepper to taste and serve at once.

Cook's Tip

Serve this quickly cooked curry with poppadoms or wholewheat chapatis or rice. A fruit chutney and side dishes of sliced banana, sliced cucumber and grated carrot will complete the main course.

Cook's Tip

This is a delicious, quick and easy-to-cook chicken dish flavoured with lemon. Serve with noodles and a green stir-fried vegetable or salad.

193 | *Chop Suey*

Preparation time
8 minutes

Cooking time
8 minutes

Serves 4

Calories
230 per portion

You will need
2 tablespoons oil
5 spring onions, chopped
2.5 cm/1 inch piece root ginger,
 peeled and chopped
2 garlic cloves, crushed
175 g/6 oz chicken breast,
 skinned and cut into thin strips
1 tablespoon tomato purée
2 tablespoons dry sherry
2 tablespoons soy sauce
1 teaspoon sugar
8 tablespoons water
275 g/10 oz beansprouts
3 eggs, beaten with 2 tablespoons
 water

Heat 1 tablespoon of the oil, add the spring onions and ginger and stir-fry for 1 minute. Add the garlic and chicken and stir-fry for 2 minutes. Lower the heat, add the tomato purée, sherry, soy sauce, sugar and 5 tablespoons of the water. Heat through gently, then transfer to a warmed serving dish.

Heat 2 teaspoons of the oil in the pan, add the beansprouts and remaining water and stir-fry for 3 minutes. Add to the serving dish and keep warm.

Wipe out the pan and heat the remaining oil. Pour in the beaten eggs and cook until set and crisp. Place on top of the beansprout mixture and serve at once.

194 | *Chicken Wings with Oyster Sauce*

Preparation time
10 minutes, plus 15
minutes marinating
time

Cooking time
about 20 minutes

Serves 4–6

Calories
200–140 per portion

You will need
450 g/1 lb chicken wings
2 tablespoons oil
2 leeks, sliced
3 tablespoons oyster sauce

For the marinade
4 spring onions, chopped
1 cm/½ inch piece root ginger,
 peeled and shredded
1 garlic clove, sliced
1 tablespoon soy sauce
2 tablespoons dry sherry

Trim the tips off the chicken wings, then cut the wings in half at the joints.

To make the marinade, mix the spring onions with the ginger, garlic, soy sauce and sherry. Add the chicken wings, stir well and leave to marinate for 15 minutes.

Heat the oil in a wok or frying pan, add the chicken and marinade and stir-fry for 15 minutes. Add the leeks and oyster sauce and cook for a further 3–4 minutes.

Serve at once, garnished with radish roses and cucumber slices if liked.

Cook's Tip

You can grow your own beansprouts by placing some beans in a jam jar. Cover with a piece of muslin and secure with an elastic band. Rinse the beans every day until the sprouts are long enough.

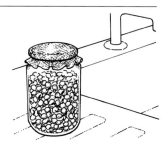

Cook's Tip

Oyster sauce is a light sauce made from oysters and soy sauce. It is often used for flavouring meat, poultry and vegetables in Chinese-style dishes.

195 | *Chicken Molee*

Preparation time
15 minutes

Cooking time
about 40 minutes

Serves 4

Calories
350 per portion

You will need
3 tablespoons oil
4 chicken breasts, skinned, boned
    and diced
6 cardamoms
6 cloves
5 cm/2 inch cinnamon stick
1 large onion, sliced
2 garlic cloves, peeled
4 cm/1½ inch piece root ginger,
    peeled and chopped
3 green chillies, seeded
juice of 1 lemon
1 teaspoon turmeric
50 g/2 oz creamed coconut
150 ml/¼ pint hot water
salt

Heat the oil in a pan, add the chicken and fry quickly on all sides to brown. Remove with a slotted spoon.

Add the cardamoms, cloves and cinnamon and fry for 1 minute. Add the onion and fry until soft.

Purée the garlic, ginger, chillies and lemon juice in a liquidizer or food processor. Add to the pan with the turmeric and cook for 5 minutes.

Melt the coconut in the hot water and add to the pan with salt to taste. Simmer for 2 minutes, then add the chicken pieces and any juices. Simmer for 15–20 minutes, until tender.

196 | *Tandoori Chicken*

Preparation time
20 minutes, plus
overnight marinating
time

Cooking time
1 hour

Oven temperature
200 C, 400 F, gas 6

Serves 4

Calories
370 per portion

You will need
½–1 teaspoon chilli powder
1 teaspoon pepper
1 teaspoon salt
2 tablespoons lemon juice
1.5 kg/3½ lb chicken, skinned
50 g/2 oz butter, melted

For the paste
4 tablespoons natural yogurt
3 garlic cloves
5 cm/2 inch piece root ginger,
    peeled
2 small dried red chillies
1 tablespoon coriander seeds
2 teaspoons cumin seeds

Mix the chilli powder, pepper, salt and lemon juice together. Slash the chicken all over and rub the mixture into the cuts; leave to stand for 1 hour.

Put all the paste ingredients in a liquidizer or food processor and work to a paste. Spread over the chicken, cover and chill overnight then bring to room temperature.

Place the chicken on a rack in a roasting pan and pour over half of the butter. Bake for 1 hour or until tender, pouring over the remaining butter after ½ hour's cooking. Serve either hot or cold.

Cook's Tip

Creamed coconut, sold as a block, is widely available and used in many Oriental dishes. It can be used in its concentrated form in a dish, or made up to make coconut milk (follow the packet instructions for good results).

Cook's Tip

Tandoori food gets its name from the clay oven, or tandoor, in which the food is traditionally cooked. Very high temperatures are reached inside the oven and food cooks quickly, preventing too much escape of moisture.

However, there isn't really enough time for the spices to penetrate the meat, so most tandoori cooked dishes are marinated before cooking to achieve good flavour.

197 | Diced Turkey with Celery

Preparation time
20 minutes, including soaking time

Cooking time
3 minutes

Serves 4

Calories
300 per portion

You will need
4 Chinese dried mushrooms
350 g/12 oz turkey breast, diced
salt
1 egg white
1 tablespoon cornflour
4 tablespoons oil
2 garlic cloves, sliced
2 slices root ginger, chopped
2 leeks, diagonally sliced
1 small head celery, diagonally sliced
1 red pepper, cored, seeded and sliced
3 tablespoons light soy sauce
2 tablespoons dry sherry
celery leaves to garnish

Soak the mushrooms in warm water for 15 minutes, squeeze dry, discard the stalks and slice the caps.

Season the turkey with salt, dip in egg white, then coat with cornflour. Heat the oil, add the turkey and stir-fry for 1 minute, until golden. Remove with a slotted spoon and set aside.

Increase the heat, add the garlic, ginger, leeks and celery and stir-fry for 1 minute. Add the turkey and red pepper and cook for 30 seconds. Stir in the soy sauce and sherry and cook for a further 30 seconds.

Spoon into a warmed serving dish and garnish with celery leaves.

Cook's Tip

This stir-fried dish is ideally cooked in a wok. If you wish to buy a wok, buy one that is made from carbon steel rather than stainless steel or aluminium which tends to scorch.

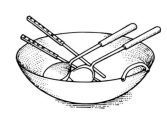

198 | Sweet and Sour Turkey

Preparation time
6 minutes

Cooking time
6 minutes

Serves 4

Calories
120 per portion

You will need
1 tablespoon oil
1 onion, finely chopped
1 turkey breast, skinned and cubed
½ yellow or red pepper, cored, seeded and sliced
3 mushrooms, sliced

For the sauce
1½ tablespoons soy sauce
1 heaped tablespoon tomato purée
2 teaspoons cornflour
300 ml/½ pint water
3 tablespoons unsweetened pineapple juice
2 tablespoons wine vinegar
1 heaped teaspoon brown sugar
spring onion fan to garnish

To make the sauce, place all the ingredients in a small pan and mix well. Bring to the boil, then simmer, stirring until thickened. Keep warm.

Heat the oil, add the onion and stir-fry for 2 minutes. Add the turkey and stir-fry for 2–3 minutes. Add the pepper and mushrooms and cook for 2–3 minutes.

Transfer to a serving dish and pour over the sauce to serve. Garnish with a spring onion fan if liked.

Cook's Tip

Serve this speedy stir-fry recipe with boiled rice and a green vegetable such as French beans or mangetout.

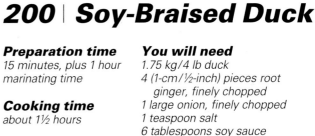

199 | *Turkey Parcels*

Preparation time
35 minutes, including
marinating time

Cooking time
5 minutes

Serves 4

Calories
300 per portion

You will need
1 tablespoon soy sauce
1 tablespoon dry sherry
1 tablespoon sesame oil
450 g/1 lb turkey breast, cut into
    16 pieces
4 spring onions, each cut into 4
    pieces
5 cm/2 inch piece root ginger,
    peeled and shredded
½ red pepper, cored, seeded and
    shredded
1 celery stick, shredded
4 tablespoons oil

Mix the soy sauce, sherry and sesame oil together, add the turkey and toss well to coat. Leave to marinate for 15–20 minutes.

Cut out 16 pieces of foil large enough to enclose the pieces of turkey generously. Brush the foil with oil, place a piece of turkey in the centre of each and top with a piece of spring onion, a little ginger, pepper and celery. Fold the foil over to enclose and seal the edges well.

Heat the oil in a wok, add the foil parcels and fry for 2 minutes on each side. Remove and leave to drain.

Reheat the oil to very hot and return the turkey parcels to the wok for 1 minute. Drain and serve.

200 | *Soy-Braised Duck*

Preparation time
15 minutes, plus 1 hour
marinating time

Cooking time
about 1½ hours

Oven temperature
220 C, 425 F, gas 7
then
190 C, 375 F, gas 5

Serves 4–6

Calories
880–590 per portion

You will need
1.75 kg/4 lb duck
4 (1-cm/½-inch) pieces root
    ginger, finely chopped
1 large onion, finely chopped
1 teaspoon salt
6 tablespoons soy sauce
3 tablespoons malt vinegar
1 tablespoon oil
4 spring onions, chopped
150 ml/¼ pint chicken stock
1 tablespoon cornflour
2 tablespoons water
1 (227-g/8-oz) can pineapple
    slices, halved, with juice
3 tablespoons dry sherry

Prick the duck skin. Mix the ginger with the onion and salt and rub inside the duck. Put in a large bowl, add the soy sauce and vinegar and leave to marinate for 1 hour, basting occasionally. Transfer to a roasting tin and roast at the higher temperature for 30 minutes.

Heat the oil in a pan, add the spring onions and fry until lightly browned. Remove and set aside. Pour off any excess fat from the duck, sprinkle with the spring onions, remaining marinade and stock. Cover and cook at the lower oven temperature for 1 hour, basting occasionally.

Remove the duck and cut into 16 pieces. Place on a warmed serving dish. Blend the cornflour with the water, then the pineapple juice. Place in a pan with the pineapple and duck juices. Cook for 2 minutes, stirring then serve with the duck. Garnish as shown.

Cook's Tip

**Turkey Parcels are a variation
of the traditional paper-
wrapped chicken, where the
food is wrapped in
greaseproof paper and fried or
steamed. Diners should
unwrap their own parcels
with their chopsticks.**

Cook's Tip

**Duck is a very fatty meat, so
the skin is pricked before
cooking to help release any
excess – this is discarded after
the first stage of cooking.**

201 | *Peking Duck*

Preparation time
20 minutes, plus
overnight hanging time

Cooking time
about 1 hour

Oven temperature
200 C, 400 F, gas 6

Serves 4

Calories
1200 per portion

You will need
1.75 kg/4 lb duck
1 tablespoon sugar
1 teaspoon salt
300 ml/½ pint water

For the sauce
3 tablespoons yellow bean sauce
2 tablespoons sugar
1 tablespoon sesame oil

For the filling
1 recipe Mandarin Pancakes (see recipe 225)
about 24 spring onion flowers
4 small leeks or spring onions, cut into strips
½ cucumber, cut into strips
½ red pepper, cored, seeded and cut into strips

Hang the duck up to dry thoroughly overnight in a cool room.

Dissolve the sugar and salt in the water and rub over the duck and leave for several hours to dry. Place on a roasting rack and roast for 1 hour.

Meanwhile, place the sauce ingredients in a pan and heat gently for 2–3 minutes, then pour into a sauce bowl.

Carve the duck into neat slices and arrange on a serving dish. Arrange the pancakes on another and garnish both with spring onion flowers. Place the leeks, cucumber and pepper on another for serving.

202 | *Braised Duck*

Preparation time
20 minutes

Cooking time
about 2¼ hours

Serves 4

Calories
650 per portion

You will need
1.75 kg/4 lb duck, cut into serving-size pieces
5 tablespoons soy sauce
4 tablespoons oil
3 spring onions, chopped
4 slices root ginger, chopped
3 star anise
1 teaspoon black peppercorns
2 teaspoons dry sherry
4 dried Chinese mushrooms, soaked for 20 minutes, drained and stemmed
100 g/4 oz canned bamboo shoots, drained and sliced
2 tablespoons cornflour
2 tablespoons water

Rub the duck with a little soy sauce. Heat the oil and fry the duck until golden on all sides. Transfer to a saucepan, add the spring onions, ginger, star anise, peppercorns, sherry, remaining soy sauce and enough water to cover. Bring to the boil, reduce the heat and simmer for 1½–2 hours, adding the mushrooms and bamboo shoots 20 minutes before the end of the cooking time.

Mix the cornflour with the water and stir into the pan and cook until thickened. Serve hot.

Cook's Tip

Peking duck is unique in Chinese cuisine, not only in the way in which it is cooked, but traditionally also for the specially reared species of ducks used, which have just the right degree of plumpness and tenderness.

The traditional way to eat this dish is to spread each pancake with a little sauce, then place a little leek and cucumber in the middle. Top with 1–2 slices of duck, roll up and eat with the fingers.

Cook's Tip

Star anise is a spice that is often used ground in Chinese 5-spice powder, but can also be bought whole. Its flavour is somewhat similar to caraway.

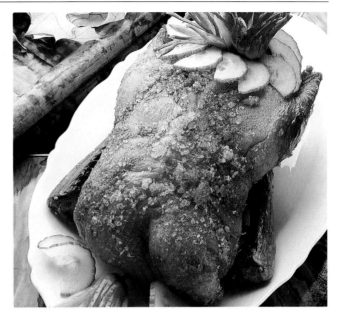

203 | *Pleasure-Boat Duck*

Preparation time
30 minutes

Cooking time
1¼–1½ hours

Oven temperature
220 C, 425 F, gas 7

Serves 4–6

Calories
800–530 per portion

You will need
1.75 kg/4 lb duck
4 dried Chinese mushrooms
2 tablespoons oil
4 spring onions, chopped
1 piece root ginger, chopped
100 g/4 oz lean pork shredded
50 g/2 oz cooked broad beans

For the glaze
3 tablespoons soy sauce
1 tablespoon dry sherry
1 tablespoon sesame oil

For the garnish
turnip flowers (see Cook's Tip)
radishes
mint leaves

Immerse the duck in a pan of boiling water for 2 minutes, then drain well. Soak the mushrooms in warm water for 15 minutes, squeeze dry, discard the stems then slice the caps.

Heat the oil, add the spring onions, ginger and pork and fry for 2 minutes. Add the beans and cook for 1 minute. Add the mushrooms and leave to cool, then use to stuff the duck and sew up securely.

Mix the glaze ingredients together and brush over the duck. Place in a roasting pan and roast for 1¼–1½ hours, basting occasionally. Transfer to a serving plate and garnish as shown. Serve at once.

204 | *Nanking Spiced Duck*

Preparation time
15 minutes, plus 3 days chilling time

Cooking time
1¼–1½ hours

Oven temperature
200 C, 400 F, gas 6

Serves 4–6

Calories
700–460 per portion

You will need
100 g/4 oz coarse salt
3 teaspoons Szechuan
   peppercorns
2 kg/4½ lb duck

For the garnish
chilli flowers (see Cook's Tip
   recipe 183)
cucumber twists and slices

Place the salt and peppercorns in a frying pan and cook over a high heat for 10 minutes to brown (see Cook's Tip). Leave to cool slightly.

Rub this mixture thoroughly over both the inside and outside of the duck. Wrap lightly in foil and store in the refrigerator for 3 days.

Remove the foil and place on a rack in a roasting pan. Roast for 1¼–1½ hours until golden.

Transfer to a warmed serving dish and garnish with chilli flowers and cucumber twists and slices.

Cook's Tip

To make turnip flowers, thinly pare a strip from a whole peeled turnip, taking care to keep it in one piece. Tightly curl into a circle to make a flower.

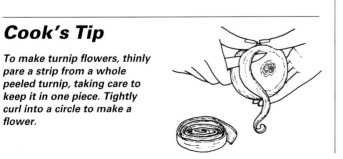

Cook's Tip

Take care when frying the salt and peppercorns that the mixture just browns and does not burn, or the mixture will give a bitter taste to the duck.

Rice, Noodles and Breads

Few dishes in China are served without a bowl of boiled, steamed or fried rice, noodles or dumplings; and the Indians rarely, if ever, feast without a hefty helping of Basmati or pilau rice, or a generous wedge of naan, chapati, puri, paratha or poppadom.

205 | Parent-Child Bowl

(Illustrated on back jacket)

Preparation time
20 minutes, plus 1 hour draining time

Cooking time
about 25 minutes

Serves 4

Calories
640 per portion

You will need
500 g/1 lb 2 oz short-grain rice
400 ml/14 fl oz Dashi/soup stock (see Cook's Tip recipe 235)
5 tablespoons soy sauce
2 tablespoons sake (rice wine)
1 tablespoon mirin (sweet rice wine)
1 tablespoon sugar
2 medium onions, sliced
225 g/8 oz boneless chicken meat, skinned and chopped
4 spring onions
4 eggs, beaten

Wash the rice, drain in a sieve for 1 hour. Place in a pan, add 685 ml/23 fl oz cold water. Bring to the boil, lower the heat, cover and simmer for 15 minutes. Remove and leave tightly covered for 10–15 minutes.

Mix the stock with the soy sauce, sake, mirin and sugar. Pour ¼ into a frying pan. Add ¼ of the onions, bring to the boil then add ¼ of the chicken meat and cook for 2 minutes.

Meanwhile, cut the spring onions in half lengthways, reserve the green part then slice the remainder into 6-cm/2-inch lengths. Add ¼ of the spring onions to the stock mixture, cook for a few seconds, then pour over ¼ of the beaten eggs. Cook until only just set. Remove and repeat to make 4 'omelettes'.

To serve, divide the hot rice equally between 4 individual plates, top each with an 'omelette' and garnish with the reserved spring onion.

206 | Turmeric Rice

Preparation time
20 minutes

Cooking time
20–25 minutes

Serves 8

Calories
370 per portion

You will need
4 tablespoons oil
2 onions, thinly sliced
2 garlic cloves, crushed
450 g/1 lb long-grain rice
1 teaspoon turmeric
300 ml/½ pint coconut milk (see Cook's Tip recipe 2)
1–2 stems lemon grass, bruised (see Cook's Tip)
salt

For the garnish
1 chilli flower (see Cook's Tip recipe 183)
1 plain omelette, made with 1 egg, cut into strips
cucumber chunks

Heat the oil in a large pan, add the onions and garlic and fry gently until soft. Stir in the rice and turmeric and stir well. Add the coconut milk and 900 ml/1½ pints cold water, then the lemon grass and salt to taste. Bring to the boil, cover and cook over a gentle heat for 15–20 minutes, until all the liquid has been absorbed. Remove from the heat and leave to stand for 15 minutes.

Mound on to a warmed serving plate, garnish with the chilli flower, omelette strips and cucumber chunks.

Cook's Tip

Parent-Child Bowl is a direct translation of this Japanese dish, and the dish is so named because it combines both chicken and egg. In Japan a special Oyako Donburi frying pan is used, but a pancake or frying pan can be used **successfully. Garnish with watercress sprigs and a tomato rose if liked.**

Cook's Tip

Lemon grass is an aromatic grass native to South-east Asia. 'Bruising' it helps let out the aroma – do this by mixing lightly in a pestle and mortar. Lemon grass is also available in powdered form, known as Sereh powder.

207 | *Plain Boiled Rice*

Preparation time
*35 minutes, including
soaking time*

You will need
*350 g/12 oz long-grain rice
450 g/¾ pint water
salt*

Cooking time
20–25 minutes

Serves 4

Calories
300 per portion

Wash the rice thoroughly under cold running water, then soak in cold water for 30 minutes; drain.

Place the rice in a pan with the water and salt to taste, bring to the boil, cover and simmer very gently for 20–25 minutes, until the rice is tender and the liquid absorbed. If cooking on an electric hob, the heat can be turned off once the rice has come to the boil.

Transfer the rice to a warmed serving dish. Serve as an accompaniment to curries and other spicy dishes.

208 | *Tomato Rice*

Preparation time
*35 minutes, including
soaking time*

You will need
*225 g/8 oz long-grain rice
3 tablespoons oil
1 onion, sliced
1 garlic clove, crushed
2.5 cm/1 inch piece root ginger,
   peeled and chopped
1 (539-g/1 lb 3-oz) can tomatoes
salt
2 tablespoons finely chopped
   fresh coriander leaves*

Cooking time
20–25 minutes

Serves 4

Calories
320 per portion

Wash the rice thoroughly under cold running water, then soak in cold water for 30 minutes; drain.

Heat the oil in a large pan, add the onion and fry until golden. Add the garlic and ginger and fry for 2 minutes. Add the rice, stir well and fry for 2 minutes.

Break up the tomatoes in their juice and add to the rice with salt to taste. Bring to the boil, then cover and simmer for 15–20 minutes, until tender.

Transfer to a warmed serving dish and sprinkle with the coriander.

Cook's Tip

Successful rice cooking is essential for ethnic meals. The best rice for Indian meals is undoubtedly Basmati, although Patna rice can also be used. There are many different methods for cooking rice, but one of the most **important things to remember is to wash the rice thoroughly before cooking. This helps to prevent the grains of rice from sticking together during cooking.**

Cook's Tip

It is now possible to buy tomatoes flavoured with herbs or spices – they may be used instead of the plain canned tomatoes in this recipe.

209 | *Pilau Rice*

Preparation time
*10 minutes, plus 30
minutes soaking time*

Cooking time
about 20 minutes

Serves 4

Calories
310 per portion

You will need
*225 g/8 oz long-grain rice
3 tablespoons oil
5 cm/2 inch cinnamon stick
4 cardamom seeds
4 cloves
1 onion, sliced
600 ml/1 pint beef stock or water
salt*

For the garnish
*lemon or lime slices
dill or fennel sprigs*

Wash the rice thoroughly under cold running water, then soak in cold water for 30 minutes; drain.

Heat the oil in a pan, add the cinnamon, cardamoms and cloves and fry for a few seconds. Add the onion and fry until golden.

Add the rice and fry, stirring occasionally, for 5 minutes. Add the stock or water and salt to taste. Bring to the boil, then simmer, uncovered, for 10 minutes, until the rice is tender and the liquid absorbed.

Transfer to a warmed serving dish and garnish with lime or lemon slices and herb sprigs.

210 | *Coconut Rice*

Preparation time
*35 minutes, including
soaking time*

Cooking time
20–25 minutes

Serves 4

Calories
340 per portion

You will need
*350 g/12 oz Basmati rice
450 ml/¾ pint thin coconut milk
(see Cook's Tip recipe 2)
½ teaspoon turmeric
8 shallots, coarsely chopped
20 peppercorns
1 teaspoon salt*

Wash the rice thoroughly under cold running water, then soak for 30 minutes; drain.

Put the coconut milk in a pan, stir in the turmeric, then add the rice. Bring to the boil, then cover and simmer gently for about 10 minutes. Add the shallots, peppercorns and salt and continue cooking gently for another 10 minutes or until the rice is tender. Be careful not to let the rice burn.

Transfer to a warmed serving dish and serve at once.

Cook's Tip

This basic recipe can also be used to make vegetable pilau. Add 100 g/4 oz each shelled peas, thinly sliced carrots and cauliflower florets to the pan after frying the onion. Fry for 5 minutes, then add the rice and cook as above.

Cook's Tip

Coconut-flavoured rice from southern India makes a change from plain boiled rice. It can be garnished with a few chopped spring onions, both the green and white parts, or with tiny prawns, rubbed over with salt and chilli powder and then quickly fried in a little hot oil until pink and cooked through.

211 | *Vegetable Rice*

Preparation time
10 minutes

Cooking time
15–20 minutes

Serves 4–6

Calories
280–190 per portion

You will need
2 tablespoons oil
2 leeks, washed and sliced
1 cm/½ inch slice root ginger,
    peeled and finely chopped
1 garlic clove, thinly sliced
225 g/8 oz long-grain rice
salt
225 g/8 oz spring greens,
    shredded

Heat the oil in a wok or deep frying pan, add the leeks, ginger and garlic and fry quickly for 30 seconds. Add the rice, stirring to coat each grain with the oil mixture. Add sufficient boiling water just to cover the rice. Season to taste with salt. Bring to the boil, cover and simmer for 5 minutes.

Add the spring greens, bring back to the boil and simmer for 7–9 minutes until the rice is tender. Drain and serve at once.

212 | *Fried Rice*

Preparation time
15 minutes, plus 1 hour
soaking time

Cooking time
about 40 minutes

Serves 4

Calories
420 per portion

You will need
350 g/12 oz long-grain rice
450 ml/¾ pint water
salt
2 tablespoons vegetable oil
4 shallots or 1 onion, thinly sliced
2 red chillies, seeded and thinly
    sliced
50 g/2 oz chopped pork, beef or
    bacon
1 tablespoon light soy sauce
1 teaspoon tomato paste

For the garnish
few fried onion slices
1 plain omelette, made with 1 egg,
    cut into strips
few fresh coriander leaves
few cucumber slices

Prepare and cook the rice as for Plain Boiled Rice (see recipe 207).

Heat the oil in a wok or frying pan, add the shallots and chillies and fry for 1–3 minutes. Add the meat or bacon and fry for 3 minutes, stirring constantly. Add the rice, soy sauce and tomato paste and stir-fry for 5–8 minutes, then season with salt to taste.

Transfer to a warmed serving dish and garnish with the onion, omelette, coriander and cucumber. Serve at once.

Cook's Tip

In India, 275–350 g/11–12 oz raw rice is normally served per person. People in the West however, find it difficult to ingest such large amounts, so 50–100 g/2–4 oz raw rice per person is usually allowed.

Cook's Tip

The ingredients in this recipe for Fried Rice, or Nasi Goreng, can be varied according to taste and availability. It is usually eaten with meat or fish and vegetables and is particularly popular served with baked or grilled fish, or any kind of saté. The chillies in this recipe give the rice a good red colour but they do make it hot – substitute ground paprika for a milder rice.

213 | Fried Rice with Ham and Beansprouts

Preparation time
15 minutes

Cooking time
8–10 minutes

Serves 4

Calories
280 per portion

You will need
2 tablespoons vegetable oil
2 spring onions, finely chopped
1 garlic clove, crushed
350 g/12 oz cooked long-grain rice (see Rice recipe 207)
175 g/6 oz cooked ham, diced
2 tablespoons soy sauce
2 eggs
salt and pepper
225 g/8 oz fresh or canned beansprouts, drained

Heat the oil in a pan. Add the spring onions and garlic and stir-fry for 2 minutes. Add the rice and stir well. Cook gently, turning, until heated through.

Stir in the ham and soy sauce. Beat the eggs with salt and pepper to taste. Pour into the rice mixture in a thin stream, stirring all the time. Add the beansprouts and continue cooking, stirring, until all the ingredients are hot and the eggs are set. Serve at once.

214 | Kitcheree

Preparation time
15 minutes, plus 1 hour soaking time

Cooking time
40–55 minutes

Serves 4

Calories
580 per portion

You will need
225 g/8 oz Basmati rice
225 g/8 oz yellow moong dhal lentils
1 garlic clove, sliced
5 cloves
5 cardamom seeds
5 cm/2 inch cinnamon stick
75 g/3 oz ghee
1 small onion, sliced
1 teaspoon turmeric
½ teaspoon salt

For the garnish
fried onion rings
chopped fresh coriander leaves

Mix the rice and dhal together and wash thoroughly in cold water, then leave to soak in cold water for 1 hour.

Fry the garlic, cloves, cardamoms and cinnamon in the ghee in a large pan for 1 minute. Add the onion and fry for a further 1 minute. Drain the rice and lentils and add to the pan with the turmeric and salt. Toss gently over a low heat for 4–5 minutes.

Pour over enough boiling water to cover the rice plus 2.5 cm/1 inch, cover with a tight-fitting lid and simmer for 30–45 minutes until the rice is cooked and all the liquid has been absorbed.

Transfer to a warmed serving dish and garnish with fried onion rings and chopped coriander.

Cook's Tip

This is a good dish to prepare in advance – simply prepare all the cooked ingredients in advance then chill, then stir-fry the cooked ingredients at the last possible moment before serving, for freshness.

Cook's Tip

Kitcheree is a dish prepared with rice and lentils. It must be stressed that any spicing is to enhance the flavour of these two ingredients. The above recipe is a good general one, making use of the yellow moong dhal variety of lentils.

Kitcheree is the dish from which the idea for that favourite breakfast dish, Kedgeree, developed.

215 | *Mixed Seafood Stick Noodles*

Preparation time
about 15 minutes

Cooking time
about 15 minutes

Serves 4–6

Calories
550–360 per portion

You will need
4 dried Chinese mushrooms (see
    Cook's Tip)
450 g/1 lb rice stick noodles (see
    Cook'sTip)
salt
2 tablespoons oil
4 spring onions, chopped
2 garlic cloves, sliced
5 cm/2 inch piece root ginger,
    peeled and finely chopped
50 g/2 oz peeled prawns
100 g/4 oz squid, sliced (optional)
1 (225-g/7½-oz) can clams,
    drained
2 tablespoons dry sherry
1 tablespoon soy sauce

Soak the mushrooms in warm water for 15 minutes. Squeeze well, discard the stalks, then slice the mushroom caps.

Cook the noodles in boiling salted water for 7–8 minutes until just tender. Drain and rinse in cold water. Set aside.

Heat the oil in a wok or deep frying pan, add the spring onions, garlic and ginger and stir-fry for 30 seconds. Stir in the mushrooms, prawns and squid, if using, then cook for 2 minutes. Stir in the remaining ingredients, then carefully stir in the noodles and heat through.

Pile the mixture into a warmed serving dish and serve at once.

Cook's Tip

Dried Chinese mushrooms are available from specialist shops. They must be soaked in warm water for at least 15 minutes before using and the stalks must be removed before use. Continental dried mushrooms can be used instead, if preferred.

Rice stick noodles are long sticks, like noodles, made from rice flour. They do not require soaking before use.

216 | *Noodles Tossed with Meat and Vegetables*

Preparation time
20 minutes

Cooking time
about 5 minutes

Serves 4–6

Calories
550–360 per portion

You will need
2 carrots, peeled
3 celery sticks
½ cucumber
2 green chillies, seeded
2 tablespoons oil
1 garlic clove, chopped
350 g/12 oz minced pork
4 spring onions, sliced
1 small green pepper, cored,
    seeded and sliced
1 tablespoon soy sauce
2 tablespoons sweet red bean
    paste (see Cook's Tip)
1 tablespoon dry sherry
350 g/12 oz noodles, cooked

Cut the carrots, celery and cucumber into matchstick lengths. Slice the chillies finely.

Heat the oil in a wok or deep frying pan, add the chillies and garlic and fry quickly for about 30 seconds. Add the pork and cook for 2 minutes. Increase the heat, add the vegetables and cook for 1 minute. Stir in the soy sauce, red bean paste, sherry and noodles. Stir well to mix and heat through.

Pile on to a warmed serving dish and serve at once.

Cook's Tip

Sweet red bean paste is a thick red paste made from soya beans with added sugar and is sold in cans. It is generally used as a dip or as a base for sweet sauces.

217 | Crispy Fried Noodles

Preparation time
15 minutes

Cooking time
about 15 minutes

Serves 4–6

Calories
500–330 per portion

You will need
3 celery sticks
100 g/4 oz spinach leaves,
    washed
450 g/1 lb egg noodles
salt
1 tablespoon oil
1 garlic clove, sliced
5 cm/2 inch piece root ginger,
    peeled and finely chopped
3 spring onions, chopped
100 g/4 oz lean pork, sliced
100 g/4 oz boned chicken breast
    meat, shredded
1 tablespoon soy sauce
1 tablespoon dry sherry
50 g/2 oz peeled prawns

Slice the celery sticks diagonally and shred the spinach leaves.

Cook the noodles in boiling salted water according to the packet instructions until just tender; do not overcook. Drain and rinse with cold water.

Heat the oil in a wok or deep frying pan, add the garlic, ginger and spring onions and fry for 1 minute. Add the pork and chicken and stir-fry for 2 minutes. Add the noodles and remaining ingredients and cook for 3 minutes.

Pile on to a warmed serving dish and serve at once.

218 | Dan-Dan Noodles

Preparation time
15 minutes

Cooking time
about 20 minutes

Serves 4

Calories
500 per portion

You will need
450 g/1 lb noodles
salt
2 tablespoons tahini or sesame
    seed paste
6 spring onions, chopped
2 garlic cloves, crushed
5 cm/2 inch piece root ginger,
    peeled and finely chopped
1 tablespoon soy sauce
2 teaspoons red wine vinegar
900 ml/1½ pints beef or chicken
    stock
2 teaspoons hot pepper oil (see
    Cook's Tip – optional)

Cook the noodles in boiling salted water according to the packet instructions, until just tender. Drain and keep hot.

Blend the sesame seed paste with 4 tablespoons water and place in a pan, together with the remaining ingredients, except the stock and pepper oil. Cook over a moderate heat, stirring frequently, for about 5 minutes.

Meanwhile, bring the stock to the boil and simmer for 2 minutes. Divide the noodles and hot sauce between 4 individual soup bowls. Spoon over the hot stock and top with the hot pepper oil, if using. Serve at once.

Cook's Tip

There are many different kinds of soy sauce available, both light and dark – the common dark variety is the one used mainly for cooking (unless otherwise stated) while the light kind is generally used as an accompaniment.

Cook's Tip

Hot pepper oil is a hot tasting oil made from hot chilli peppers. It should be used sparingly.

219 | Naan

Preparation time
2¼ hours, including
resting time

Cooking time
10 minutes

Oven temperature
240 C, 475 F, gas 9

Makes 6

Calories
360 per naan

You will need
15 g/½ oz fresh yeast
¼ teaspoon sugar
2 tablespoons warm water
450 g/1 lb self-raising flour
1 teaspoon salt
150 ml/¼ pint tepid milk
150 ml/¼ pint natural yogurt (at
    room temperature)
2 tablespoons melted butter or
    cooking oil

For the garnish
2–3 tablespoons melted butter
1 tablespoon poppy or sesame
    seeds

Mix the yeast with the sugar and water and leave in a warm place for 15 minutes.

Sift the flour and salt into a bowl, make a well in the centre and pour in the yeast liquid, milk, yogurt and butter or oil. Mix to a smooth dough and knead for 10 minutes until smooth and elastic. Place in a bowl, cover and leave to rise in a warm place for 1–1½ hours.

Knead on a floured surface, then divide into 6 pieces. Pat or roll each piece into an oval. Place on warmed baking trays and bake for 10 minutes. Brush with the melted butter and sprinkle with the poppy or sesame seeds. Serve warm.

220 | Puri

Preparation time
about 20 minutes, plus
30 minutes standing
time

Cooking time
about 5–10 minutes

Makes 16

Calories
100 per puri

You will need
225 g/8 oz wholemeal flour
¼ teaspoon salt
about 150 ml/¼ pint warm water
2 teaspoons melted ghee
oil for deep frying

Mix the flour with the salt in a bowl. Make a well in the centre, add the water gradually and work to a dough. Knead in the ghee, then knead for 10 minutes, until smooth and elastic. Cover and set aside for 30 minutes.

Divide the dough into 16 pieces. With lightly oiled hands, pat each piece into a ball. Lightly oil a pastry board and rolling pin and roll out each ball into a thin circular pancake.

Deep fry the puris very quickly, turning them over once, until deep golden in colour. Drain well and serve at once, hot.

Cook's Tip

Naan is a north Indian bread traditionally baked in a clay oven called a tandoor. The leavened dough is rolled or slapped into an oval shape, then stuck inside the heated oven so that it hangs free; its weight stretches the naan into **a teardrop shape. It is usually served with tandoori chicken and kebabs, but is good with any of the drier curries.**

Cook's Tip

Puris are delicious served with vegetable curries. They can be made with half wholemeal and half plain white flour if preferred.

221 | Chapati

Preparation time
45 minutes, including
resting time

Cooking time
12 minutes

Makes 12

Calories
65 per chapati

You will need
225 g/8 oz wholewheat flour
1 teaspoon salt
200 ml/⅓ pint water

Place the flour and salt in a bowl. Make a well in the centre and gradually stir in the water. Work to a soft, supple dough. Knead for 10 minutes, then cover and leave in a cool place for 30 minutes. Knead again very thoroughly, then divide into 12 pieces. Roll out each piece on a floured surface into a thin round pancake.

Lightly grease a griddle or heavy-based frying pan with a little ghee or oil and place over a moderate heat. Add a chapati and cook until blisters appear. Press down with a fish slice, then turn and cook the other side until lightly coloured. Remove from the pan and keep warm while cooking the rest.

Brush a little butter on one side, fold into quarters and serve warm.

222 | Chapati with Onion

Preparation time
45 minutes, including
resting time

Cooking time
45 minutes

Makes 12

Calories
100 per chapati

You will need
225 g/8 oz wholewheat flour
1 teaspoon salt
about 200 ml/⅓ pint water
4 teaspoons ghee or unsalted
    butter, melted
2 onions
2 green chillies
½ teaspoon salt

Make the dough as for Chapati (see recipe 221), adding 2 teaspoons of the ghee or melted butter to the mixture.

Peel the onions, then chop the onions and chillies very finely. Stir in the salt. Place in a sieve and squeeze out any liquid.

Divide the dough into 12 pieces. Roll out each piece on a floured surface into a thin round. Put a little of the onion and chilli mixture in the centre, fold the dough over and form into a ball, then roll out carefully into a round.

Cook as for Chapati (see recipe 00), using the remaining ghee or butter to grease the pan.

Cook's Tip

The Chapati is the daily bread of millions of Indians. It is usually made from finely ground wholewheat flour but can also be made from a mixture of white and wholewheat, or from barley, millet, maize or chickpea flour.

Cook's Tip

Flavoured chapatis are excellent. Any kind of vegetable can be used, as long as it is mashed and spiced. Use only a small amount, or it will break through the dough. Chopped herbs like mint and coriander with green chillies are easier to use and very tasty.

223 | *Paratha*

Preparation time
1 hour, including resting time

Cooking time
15 minutes

Makes 6

Calories
250 per paratha

You will need
*225 g/8 oz wholewheat flour
1 teaspoon salt
200 ml/⅓ pint water
50–75 g/2–3 oz ghee or butter, melted*

Make the dough as for Chapati (see recipe 221) and divide into 6 pieces. Roll out each piece on a floured surface into a thin circle. Brush with melted butter or ghee and fold in half; brush again and fold in half again. Roll out again to a circle about 3 mm/⅛ inch thick.

Lightly grease a griddle or heavy-based frying pan with a little ghee or butter and place over a moderate heat. Add a paratha and cook for 1 minute. Lightly brush the top with a little melted butter or ghee and turn over. Brush all round the edge with melted butter or ghee and cook until golden. Remove from the pan and keep warm while cooking the rest. Serve warm.

224 | *Poppadoms*

Preparation time
about 30 minutes

Cooking time
2–2½ hours drying time then about 5 minutes

Oven temperature
180 C, 350 F, gas 4

Makes about 20

Calories
150 per poppadom

You will need
*450 g/1 lb urhad/lentil flour
4½ teaspoons salt
1 tablespoon baking powder
about 50 g/2 oz ghee
2 teaspoons black peppercorns
vegetable oil for frying*

Sift the flour, salt and baking powder into a bowl and gradually add 250 ml/8 fl oz tepid water to form a very hard dough.

Melt the ghee, knead the dough for at least 20 minutes, sprinkling it with enough melted ghee to prevent it sticking. Crush the peppercorns and sprinkle over the dough, then knead until evenly distributed.

Break into about 20 pieces, roll out very thinly until 15 cm/6 inches in diameter. Stack on top of each other between sheets of greaseproof paper, then dry out in the oven for 2–2½ hours.

To cook, heat the oil in a deep frying pan until hot. Add the poppadoms, two at a time and fry for about 5–10 seconds, then turn them over and cook for a further 5–10 seconds (frying two together prevents them from curling up). Drain on absorbent kitchen paper.

Cook's Tip

The Paratha is a fancy chapati, layered with fat like puff pastry – very delicious, but very fattening!

Cook's Tip

Ideally poppadoms should be served within 1 hour of frying, but they can be kept crisp, or be re-crisped in a hot oven.

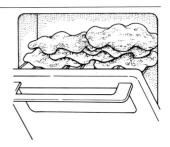

225 | *Mandarin Pancakes*

Preparation time
20 minutes

Cooking time
about 15–20 minutes

Makes 24

Calories
160 per 2 pancakes

You will need
450 g/1 lb plain flour
300 ml/½ pint boiling water
1 teaspoon salt
vegetable oil

Sift the flour into a bowl. Mix the water with the salt and gradually stir into the flour. Mix to make a firm dough. Divide into 24 pieces and press each into a flat pancake with the palm of your hand. Brush one pancake with a little oil, then top with a second to make a 'sandwich'. Repeat to make a total of 12 'sandwiches'. Roll out each to make a 15-cm/6-inch circle.

Heat an ungreased frying pan over a moderate heat and, when hot, fry the 'sandwiches', one at a time, until bubbles appear on the surface. Turn over and cook until the underside has brown spots. Remove from the pan and peel the pancakes apart for serving. Fold into quarters for serving.

226 | *Crispy Pancake Rolls*

Preparation time
10 minutes

Cooking time
45 minutes

Serves 4–6

Calories
350–230 per portion

You will need
225 g/8 oz plain flour
pinch of salt
1 egg
about 300 ml/½ pint water

For the filling
1 tablespoon oil
1 teaspoon root ginger, chopped
2 garlic cloves, crushed
225 g/8 oz chicken breast, skinned and diced
2 tablespoons soy sauce
1 tablespoon dry sherry
100 g/4 oz mushrooms, sliced
3 spring onions, chopped
50 g/2 oz peeled prawns

Sift the flour and salt into a bowl, add the egg and beat in sufficient water to make a smooth batter. Use to make thin pancakes in a 20-cm/8-inch frying pan.

To make the filling, heat the oil in a wok or frying pan, add the ginger and garlic and fry for 30 seconds. Add the chicken and brown quickly. Stir in the soy sauce and sherry, then the mushrooms and spring onions. Increase the heat and cook for 1 minute. Remove from the heat, stir in the prawns and cool.

Place 2–3 tablespoons of the filling in the centre of each pancake. Fold in the sides and form into a tight roll, sealing the edge with a little flour and water paste. Deep fry the rolls a few at a time for 2–3 minutes. Drain on absorbent kitchen paper, then serve.

Cook's Tip

Mandarin pancakes are traditionally served with Peking Duck (see recipe 201). They are spread with sauce and topped with shredded cucumber, leek or spring onion and rolled up for eating.

Cook's Tip

Deep-frying is a popular Chinese cooking technique and used to cook stuffed pancakes called spring rolls. The chicken in this recipe could be replaced with shredded cooked pork, beef or turkey.

227 | Fried Wonton with Sweet and Sour Sauce

Preparation time
20 minutes

Cooking time
about 20 minutes

Serves 4–6

Calories
650–450 per portion
(sauce – whole recipe
250)

You will need
450 g/1 lb wonton skins
3 tablespoons soy sauce
1 tablespoon dry sherry
450 g/1 lb minced pork
1 teaspoon brown sugar
1 garlic clove, crushed
2.5 cm/1 inch piece root ginger,
   peeled and finely chopped
225 g/8 oz frozen spinach,
   thawed and squeezed dry
oil for deep frying

For the sauce
(see Cook's Tip)

Cut out 5-cm/2-inch squares from the wonton skins. Put the soy sauce, sherry and pork in a bowl and mix well. Add the sugar, garlic, ginger and spinach and mix well. Spoon a little of this mixture on to the centre of each wonton skin. Dampen the edges and fold to form triangles, pressing the edges firmly together to ensure that the filling does not come out during frying.

   Heat the oil and fry the wonton, a few at a time, for about 5 minutes until golden. Drain on absorbent kitchen paper and serve hot with sweet and sour sauce (see Cook's Tip).

228 | Fried Steamed Dumplings

Preparation time
20 minutes

Cooking time
25–26 minutes

Serves 4–6

Calories
630–440 per portion

You will need
450 g/1 lb self-raising flour
pinch of salt
200–250 ml/7–8 fl oz water
oil for deep frying
350 g/12 oz minced pork
1 tablespoon soy sauce
1 tablespoon dry sherry
2 teaspoons sesame oil
2 spring onions, finely chopped
5 cm/2 inch piece root ginger,
   peeled and finely chopped
100 g/4 oz canned bamboo
   shoots, drained and chopped

Sift the flour and salt into a bowl. Add sufficient water to mix to a firm dough. Divide in half and knead each piece, then form into a roll 5 cm/2 inches in diameter. Slice each roll into 14 pieces and roll out each to a 7.5-cm/3-inch circle.

   Mix all the filling ingredients together and divide between the rounds, placing it in the centre. Gather the sides of the dough up around the filling to meet at the top, then firmly twist the top of the dough to close tightly. Arrange in a piece of moist muslin in a steamer and steam for 20 minutes. Drain.

   Heat the oil in a wok or deep frier, add the dumplings and fry for 5-6 minutes until golden. Drain on absorbent kitchen paper. Serve at once.

Cook's Tip

To make a sweet and sour sauce for this recipe, heat 1 tablespoon of oil in a pan, add 2 crushed garlic cloves and fry for 1 minute. Stir in 2 tablespoons each of soy sauce, clear honey, wine vinegar and tomato purée.

Add 2 teaspoons each of chilli sauce, dry sherry and cornflour (mix the cornflour with a little cold water first). Bring to the boil, cook for 2 minutes and serve hot with the cooked wonton.

Cook's Tip

Sesame oil made from sesame seeds is a nutty-flavoured oil, generally used in small quantities at the end of cooking for flavouring purposes, or for stir-frying.

Salads and Side Dishes

In the Orient, a dish without accompaniments is like an oil painting without a frame. Salads and fruit dishes offer a texture and flavour contrast to the main meal, while chutneys, pickles and sambals sweeten, spice and extend the flavours of the meal.

229 | Vinegared Cucumber

(Illustrated on back jacket)

Preparation time
20 minutes

Serves 4

Calories
40 per portion

You will need
1 large or 2 small cucumbers
1 teaspoon salt
15 g/½ oz wakame or dried young
 seaweed
2.5–4 cm/1–1½ inch piece root
 ginger, peeled and shredded

For the Saubaizu sauce
3 tablespoons rice vinegar
1 tablespoon soy sauce
1 tablespoon sugar
¼–½ teaspoon salt

Halve the cucumber lengthways; remove the seeds, then slice very thinly. Sprinkle with salt, then squeeze with your hands and rinse under cold water.

Put the wakame in a bowl and cover with cold water, leave to soak for 5–10 minutes. Drain, rinse in boiling water, then rinse in cold running water. Drain well and squeeze with the hands, then cut into 2.5-cm/1-inch lengths.

Place the ginger in a bowl of ice-cold water to crisp. Put all the ingredients for the sauce in a bowl, mix well then add the cucumber and wakame and toss well.

Transfer the salad to individual salad bowls, shaping it into neat mounds. Drain the ginger and sprinkle over the top. Serve cold.

230 | Raita

Preparation time
10 minutes, plus 30 minutes standing time

Serves 4

Calories
20 per portion

You will need
100 g/4 oz cucumber, thinly sliced
salt
300 g/10 oz natural yogurt
50 g/2 oz spring onions, thinly
 sliced
1 green chilli, seeded and finely
 chopped
fresh coriander or mint leaves to
 garnish

Put the cucumber into a colander, sprinkle with salt and leave to drain for 30 minutes. Dry thoroughly.

Mix the yogurt with salt to taste and fold in the cucumber, spring onions and chilli. Arrange in a serving dish and chill until required.

Garnish with coriander or mint leaves to serve.

Cook's Tip

This classic Japanese salad of finely sliced cucumber and soft seaweed can be served as an hors d'oeuvre or as a refreshing accompaniment to a main meal.

Cook's Tip

Raita can be made with other vegetables and with fruit – bananas are particularly good.

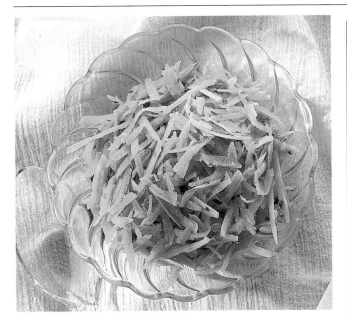

231 | *Carrot Salad*

Preparation time
10 minutes, plus 1–2
hours chilling time

Serves 4

Calories
10 per portion

You will need
100 g/4 oz carrots, peeled and
  grated
25 g/1 oz grated onion
½ tablespoon grated root ginger
1 tablespoon finely chopped mint
½ teaspoon salt
½ teaspoon sugar
1 tablespoon lemon juice

Mix all the ingredients together in a bowl, cover and chill
for 1–2 hours before serving.

232 | *Pickled Salad*

Preparation time
15 minutes, plus 5
hours standing time

Serves 4–6

Calories
100–65 per portion

You will need
450 g/1 lb cucumber, peeled
450 g/1 lb cabbage, cored and
  chopped
2 teaspoons salt
1 teaspoon crushed garlic
1 teaspoon ground Szechuan or
  black peppercorns
1 teaspoon sugar
1 tablespoon soy sauce
2 tablespoons sesame oil
1 tablespoon red wine vinegar

Crush the cucumbers until cracks appear on the surface.
Quarter lengthways, then cut into pieces. Place in a bowl
with the cabbage, sprinkle with salt and leave for 2 hours.
  Rinse the vegetables and drain on absorbent kitchen
paper. Mix together the garlic, pepper, sugar, soy sauce,
oil and vinegar. Pour over the vegetables, mix well and
allow to stand for at least 3 hours before serving. Serve
on a cabbage-lined plate if liked.

Cook's Tip

*Indian salads are invariably
chopped and mixed with
various spices – this recipe is
something of an exception
since the flavourings are mild
and feature herbs. You can of
course try using grated
celeriac instead of the carrots*
*or vary the herbs – try
coriander, chervil or parsley
instead of the mint.*

Cook's Tip

*Szechuan pepper, also sold as
anise pepper, is one of the 5
spices used in Chinese 5-spice
powder. It can be bought from
specialist shops. If you have
difficulty obtaining it then use
ordinary black pepper instead.*

233 | Spinach Salad with Cockles and Mustard Sauce

Preparation time
15 minutes

Cooking time
about 5 minutes

Serves 4

Calories
100 per portion

You will need
1 tablespoon sake (rice wine)
225 g/8 oz cockles, cleaned
3 tablespoons soy sauce, plus 1 teaspoon
1 teaspoon Japanese or other hot mustard
450 g/1 lb spinach leaves, washed and trimmed
salt
1 tablespoon sesame seeds to garnish

Heat the sake in a small saucepan, add the cockles and heat through. Drain the cockles, reserving the juice.

Put 3 tablespoons soy sauce and the mustard in a bowl and mix together. Add the cockles. Cook the spinach leaves in lightly salted boiling water for 30 seconds, then drain and plunge immediately into a bowl of ice-cold water. Drain again and squeeze out any excess water, then pour over 1 teaspoon soy sauce.

Add the cockle juice to the cockle mixture. Arrange the spinach on a serving plate. Place the cockle mixture in the centre and garnish with sesame seeds.

Cook's Tip

Sake, a rice wine, is made by fermenting freshly steamed white rice. It is the national drink of Japan. Lower quality sake is used extensively in cooking. If rice wine is unavailable, a very dry sherry may be used instead.

234 | Kidney-Flower Salad

Preparation time
10 minutes plus 30 minutes marinating time

Cooking time
2 minutes

Serves 4

Calories
120 per portion

You will need
350 g/12 oz pigs' kidneys, skinned and split in half lengthways
1 small head celery, sliced diagonally
2 slices fresh root ginger, finely shredded
2 shallots, finely chopped

For the sauce
2 tablespoons soy sauce
1 tablespoon vinegar
1 tablespoon sesame oil
1 teaspoon chilli sauce

For the garnish (optional)
pineapple slices
radish slices
grapes

Score the surface of the kidneys in a criss-cross pattern, then cut them into pieces. Cook in boiling water for 2 minutes. Drain, rinse in cold water, then drain again and transfer to a serving plate. Arrange the celery around the cold kidneys.

Mix all the sauce ingredients together, then mix with half the ginger and shallots. Pour the sauce over the kidneys, then leave to marinate for about 30 minutes before serving.

Top with the remaining ginger and shallots. Garnish with sliced pineapple, radish and grapes. Serve cold.

Cook's Tip

Fresh root ginger, sometimes called green ginger, is used in all oriental cuisines. Peel before using then chop, slice or crush. To keep fresh, peel, wash and place in a jar; cover with pale dry sherry, seal and store in the refrigerator.

235 | Japanese Salad

Preparation time
30 minutes

Cooking time
12 minutes

Serves 4

Calories
140 per portion

You will need
½ medium carrot, peeled
1 cucumber
½ bunch spring onions
100 g/4 oz boneless chicken
1 tablespoon sake (rice wine)
15 g/½ oz dried young seaweed
shiso or lettuce leaves to serve

For the Gomadare dressing
4 tablespoons seasame seeds,
   toasted
1 small garlic clove, grated
5 tablespoons rice vinegar
3 tablespoons Dashi/soup stock
   (see Cook's Tip)
1 tablespoon soy sauce
1 tablespoon mayonnaise
pinch of chilli powder
1 teaspoon salt

To make the dressing, mix all the ingredients together in a bowl. Set aside.

To make the salad, finely shred the carrot, cucumber and spring onions and place in ice cold water to crisp.

Skin the chicken, place on a plate, sprinkle with the sake and a little salt then steam for 12 minutes until tender. Cool, then shred with the fingers.

Put the seaweed in a bowl and cover with cold water. Leave to soak for 5–10 minutes. Drain, rinse in boiling water then under cold running water. Squeeze out excess water and cut into 2.5-cm/1-inch lengths.

To serve, line a large plate with the shiso or lettuce leaves and serve as shown.

Cook's Tip

To make Dashi or soup stock place 25 g/1 oz kombu (dried kelp) in a pan, add 1 litre/1¾ pints cold water and leave to soak for 10 minutes. Bring slowly to boiling point but remove before it boils. Immediately add 25 g/1 oz katsuobushi (dried bonito flakes) and bring to a rapid boil. Boil for a few seconds only, then remove from the heat. Leave to stand for 1 minute, or until the bonito flakes sink, then strain through a tea-towel into a bowl.

236 | Serundeng

Preparation time
10 minutes

Cooking time
40 minutes

Serves 4

Calories
470 per portion

You will need
oil (see method)
175 g/6 oz unsalted peanuts
1 small onion, quartered
2 garlic cloves
1 cm/½ inch piece root ginger
½ teaspoon ground cumin
1 teaspoon ground coriander
1 tablespoon lemon juice
75 g/3 oz desiccated coconut
1 teaspoon salt
1 teaspoon sugar

Coat the base of a non-stick frying pan with oil. Heat the pan and put in the peanuts. Stir-fry the nuts until lightly browned, remove to a plate and leave to cool.

Put the onion, garlic, ginger, cumin, coriander and lemon juice in a food processor or liquidizer and work until smooth.

Put 2 tablespoons oil in the frying pan and fry the spice paste for 1 minute. Add the coconut, salt and sugar and fry over a low heat, stirring for 20–30 minutes or until crisp and golden. Transfer to small dish and leave to cool.

Mix in the peanuts and serve.

Cook's Tip

Serundeng is a relish from Indonesia and should be served in tiny portions.

237 | Guava and Yogurt Side Salad

Preparation time
about 10–15 minutes,
plus 1 hour chilling time

Cooking time
about 2–3 minutes

Serves 6

Calories
80 per portion

You will need
300 g/10 oz natural yogurt
1 tablespoon lemon juice
3 canned whole guavas, drained,
    seeded and chopped
1 tablespoon ghee or clarified
    butter
1 teaspoon mustard seeds
1 green chilli, seeded and finely
    chopped
1 teaspoon chopped fresh
    coriander to garnish

Beat the yogurt and lemon juice until smooth, then stir in the guavas.

Heat the ghee in a small frying pan, add the mustard seeds, cover and cook over a medium heat until the seeds begin to 'pop'. Remove from the heat, add the chilli and then fry gently for 10 seconds, stirring constantly.

Stir the contents of the pan into the yogurt mixture. Cover and chill for at least 1 hour. Sprinkle the salad with the coriander before serving.

238 | Brinjal Sambal

Preparation time
15 minutes

Cooking time
30 minutes

Oven temperature
180 C, 350 F, gas 4

Serves 4

Calories
40 per portion

You will need
1 large aubergine
1 small onion, finely chopped
3 green chillies, finely chopped
1 cm/½ inch piece root ginger, cut
    into fine strips
2 tablespoons thick coconut milk
    or cream (see Cook's Tip
    recipe 3)
½ teaspoon salt
juice of 1 lemon

Place the aubergine on a baking tray and bake for 30 minutes or until soft. Leave to cool slightly, then slit it open and scoop out the flesh into a bowl.

Mash the aubergine with a fork and then mix in the remaining ingredients. Taste the sambal and adjust the seasoning. Serve chilled.

Cook's Tip

Ghee or clarified butter is used to fry many ingredients for Indian cooking. It is made by melting butter and separating the fat from the solids. Ghee can be heated to much higher temperatures than ordinary butter. A vegetable ghee substitute is also available. If you are unable to obtain it try using concentrated butter.

Cook's Tip

Brinjal Sambal is a typical southern Indian relish. It is quick and easy to make and, for those who like the chilli-hot taste, it makes an exciting dip for raw vegetables.

239 | *Brinjal Pickle*

Preparation time
40 minutes, including
soaking time

Cooking time
40 minutes

Makes about
1.5 kg/3 lb

Total calories
2400

You will need
1 kg/2 lb aubergines, thinly sliced
1 tablespoon salt
300 ml/½ pint hot water
100 g/4 oz tamarind
50 g/2 oz cumin seeds
25 g/1 oz dried red chillies
50 g/2 oz root ginger, peeled and
  chopped
50 g/2 oz garlic, peeled
300 ml/½ pint vinegar
150 ml/¼ pint oil
2 teaspoons mustard seeds
225 g/8 oz sugar

Sprinkle the aubergines with the salt and leave in a colander for 30 minutes to drain.

Pour the hot water on to the tamarind and leave to soak for 20 minutes. Press through a fine sieve and set aside.

Put the cumin, chillies, ginger, garlic and 2 tablespoons of the vinegar in a food processor or liquidizer and work to a paste.

Heat the oil in a large saucepan and fry the mustard seeds until they begin to splutter. Quickly add the spice paste and fry, stirring, for 2 minutes. Add the aubergine, tamarind water, remaining vinegar and the sugar and stir well. Bring to the boil, then simmer for 30–35 minutes, until the mixture is thick and pulpy.

Leave until cold then pour into sterilized jars, cover securely with waxed discs and screw-top lids. Store in a cool place.

Cook's Tip

Brinjal Pickle is for those who like hot relishes. The chillies can be reduced, but the pickle will then lose its characteristic bite.

240 | *Coriander Chutney*

Preparation time
10 minutes, plus 1 hour
marinating time

Serves 4

Calories
70 per portion

You will need
25 g/1 oz desiccated coconut
150 ml/¼ pint natural yogurt
100 g/4 oz fresh coriander leaves
  and some fine stalks
2 green chillies
juice of 1 lemon
1 teaspoon salt
1 teaspoon sugar

Mix the coconut with the yogurt and leave to stand for 1 hour to marinate.

Place in a food processor or liquidizer with the remaining ingredients and work until smooth. Chill the chutney before serving.

Cook's Tip

Coriander Chutney goes well with most curries and snacks and is excellent in chicken sandwiches. It is best eaten fresh, but will keep in the refrigerator for a day or two.

241 | *Sambal Bajak*

Preparation time
10 minutes

Cooking time
6 minutes

Serves 4

Calories
90 per portion

You will need
2 tablespoons oil
3 small onions, finely chopped
4 garlic cloves, finely chopped
1 teaspoon blachan or shrimp
    paste (see Cook's Tip)
100 g/4 oz red chillies, chopped
4 tablespoons tamarind water or
    lime juice (see Cook's Tip
    recipe 11)
1 teaspoon salt
1 teaspoon brown sugar

Heat the oil in a small frying pan, add the onions and garlic and fry until golden brown. Add the blachan or shrimp paste and fry, stirring and mashing, for 1 minute.

Stir in the remaining ingredients and fry, stirring, for 5 minutes or until the mixture is fairly dry.

Allow to cool, then spoon into a jar. Cover and keep refrigerated until required.

242 | *Bertha's Chutney*

Preparation time
5 minutes

Cooking time
45 minutes

**Makes about
1.5 kg/3 lb**

Total calories
1800

You will need
1 kg/2 lb tomatoes, quartered
100 ml/4 fl oz vinegar
225 g/8 oz sugar
100 g/4 oz raisins
100 g/4 oz sultanas
25 g/1 oz blanched almonds,
    sliced
4 garlic cloves, finely sliced
25 g/1 oz root ginger, peeled and
    finely chopped
1 tablespoon chilli powder
½ tablespoon salt

Place the tomatoes and vinegar in a large pan and heat gently until the juice starts to run. Add the sugar and bring slowly to the boil. Simmer for 5 minutes.

Add the remaining ingredients and simmer for 30 minutes or until the mixture has thickened.

Leave until cold, then pour into sterilized jars, cover securely with waxed discs and screw-top lids. Store in a cool place.

Cook's Tip

Sambal Bajak comes from Indonesia. It is extremely pungent and should be treated with respect! It will keep for several weeks stored in a screw-topped jar in the refrigerator. The blachan or shrimp paste used in the **recipe is a strong-smelling, salty shrimp paste used throughout South-east Asia. Store in a tightly shut box. It must be well fried or wrapped in foil and roasted before use.**

Cook's Tip

Bertha's Chutney is best made when tomatoes are in full season. Dried apricots can be substituted for the raisins and sultanas, but they must be soaked overnight. If you like sweet chutney use 50 g/2 oz more sugar.

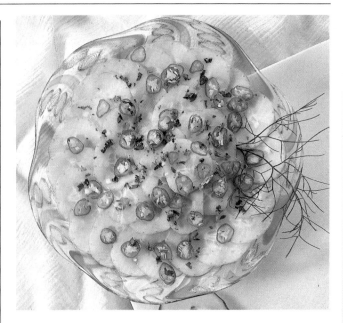

243 | Hot Relish

Preparation time
10 minutes

Cooking time
about 20–25 minutes

Serves 6–8

Calories
130–100 per portion

You will need
20 red chillies, seeded and
   chopped
10 shallots or 1 large onion,
   chopped
2 garlic cloves, chopped
5 macadamias
1 teaspoon dried shrimp paste
2 tablespoons vegetable oil
1 teaspoon grated root ginger
1 teaspoon brown sugar
3 tablespoons tamarind water
   (see Cook's Tip recipe 11)
salt
150 ml/¼ pint thick coconut milk
   or cream (see Cook's Tip
   recipe 3)

Put the chillies, shallots, garlic, macadamias and dried
shimp paste in a food processor or liquidizer and work to
a very smooth paste.

   Heat the oil in a pan, add the paste and fry for 2
minutes. Add the ginger, sugar, tamarind water and salt
to taste. Stir well, then add the coconut milk or cream.
Simmer for about 15 minutes until the sambal is thick and
oily, stirring occasionally. Increase the heat and stir-fry
for a further 2–3 minutes, then serve hot or cold.

244 | Zalata

Preparation time
15 minutes, plus 30
minutes standing time

Serves 4

Calories
10 per portion

You will need
225 g/8 oz ridge cucumbers,
   peeled and sliced
salt
1 green chilli, sliced
1 tablespoon finely chopped
   fresh coriander leaves
2 tablespoons vinegar
½ teaspoon sugar

Put the cucumber into a colander, sprinkle with salt and
leave to drain for 30 minutes. Dry thoroughly. Place in a
serving dish and add the remaining ingredients and 1 teaspoon salt. Mix well and chill thoroughly before serving.

Cook's Tip

*To chop onions or shallots,
peel then cut them in half
lengthways; place the flat side
on a chopping board. Holding
opposite sides, slice finely first
lengthways, then across.*

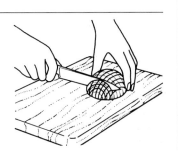

Cook's Tip

*An alternative method to the
one above is to put the
drained cucumber into a
liquidizer or food processor
with the whole chilli,
coriander leaves, sugar and
salt. Add 1 garlic clove and
just 1½ teaspoons vinegar and*
*work to a smooth paste. Chill
thoroughly before serving.*

245 | *Hot Spicy Eggs*

Preparation time
15 minutes

Cooking time
about 5 minutes

Serves 4

Calories
450 per portion

You will need
2.5 cm/1 inch cube dried shrimp
 paste (see Cook's Tip recipe
 239)
2 onions, coarsely chopped
2 garlic cloves, peeled
1 teaspoon laos powder
1–2 tablespoons sambal ulek (see
 Cook's Tip)
2–4 fresh chillies, seeded
4–6 tablespoons vegetable oil
3–4 tablespoons tomato purée
400 ml/14 fl oz stock or water
2 teaspoons tamarind, soaked in 4
 tablespoons warm water for 10
 minutes
2 teaspoons brown sugar
1–2 tablespoons coconut cream
 (see Cook's Tip recipe 3)
salt
8 hard-boiled eggs, shelled
1–2 spring onion tops, shredded

Put the shrimp paste with the onions, garlic, laos powder, sambal ulek and chillies in a food processor or liquidizer and work to a smooth paste. Heat the oil and fry the paste, without browning, until it gives off a spicy aroma. Stir in the tomato purée and stock or water then simmer, uncovered, for a few minutes.

Just before serving, strain in the tamarind water, add the sugar, coconut cream and salt to taste. Leave the eggs whole or cut in half and add to the sauce. Heat through, then transfer to a serving dish and sprinkle with the spring onions. Serve hot.

Cook's Tip

Sambal Ulek is a paste made from fresh chillies and salt. It can be purchased ready-made or prepared at home; 2 fresh chillies and ½ teaspoon salt pounded until smooth will make about 2 teaspoons.
Sambal Goreng sauce is *also useful for other ingredients besides eggs suggested here. Try it with cooked green beans, cooked chicken livers or peeled prawns.*

246 | *Coconut Relish*

Preparation time
10 minutes

Serves 4–6

Calories
110–75 per portion

You will need
1 teaspoon dried shrimp paste,
 fried or roasted (see Cook's Tip,
 recipe 239)
2 garlic cloves, chopped
3–5 hot chillies, finely chopped
1 tablespoon gula jawa or palm
 sugar (see Cook's Tip)
1 tablespoon tamarind water (see
 Cook's Tip recipe 11)
7 tablespoons freshly grated
 coconut
salt

Put the dried shrimp paste, garlic, chillies and palm sugar in a food processor or liquidizer and work to a very smooth paste.

Add the remaining ingredients, with salt to taste and mix well. Serve cold on the day of making.

Cook's Tip

Malaysian palm sugar, gula jawa, also known as gula malaka is sold in thin blocks. Brown sugar may be used as a substitute.

247 | *Dried Fruit Curry*

Preparation time
10 minutes, plus
overnight soaking time

Cooking time
40 minutes

Serves 4

Calories
220 per portion

You will need
1 onion, peeled
1 garlic clove, peeled
2.5 cm/1 inch piece root ginger,
   peeled
2 teaspoons chilli powder
2 teaspoons ground coriander
1 teaspoon salt
2 tablespoons oil
225 g/8 oz mixed dried fruit,
   excluding prunes, soaked
   overnight
juice of 1–2 lemons

Place the onion, garlic, ginger, chilli powder, coriander and salt in a food processor or liquidizer and work to a smooth paste.

Heat the oil in a pan, add the paste and fry for 3 minutes.

Drain the fruit, reserving the liquid, and cut up the larger pieces. Add to the pan and fry for 2 minutes. Make up the reserved liquid to 300 ml/½ pint with water, add to the pan and simmer for 30 minutes.

Stir in the lemon juice to taste and serve at once.

248 | *Yogurt Curry*

Preparation time
10 minutes

Cooking time
25 minutes

Serves 4

Calories
130 per portion

You will need
450 g/1 lb natural yogurt
2 tablespoons gram flour (see
   Cook's Tip recipe 13)
2 tablespoons oil
½ teaspoon ground cumin
½ teaspoon ground coriander
2 garlic cloves, crushed
3–4 green chillies, finely chopped
1 teaspoon turmeric
salt
1 tablespoon chopped fresh
   coriander leaves
6 curry leaves
fresh coriander leaves to garnish

Mix the yogurt and the gram flour together.

Heat the oil in a pan, add the cumin, ground coriander, garlic and chillies and fry for 1 minute. Stir in the turmeric, then immediately pour in the yogurt mixture. Add salt to taste and simmer, uncovered, for 10 minutes, stirring occasionally.

Add the chopped coriander and the curry leaves and continue cooking for a further 10 minutes. Transfer to a warmed serving dish and garnish with coriander leaves to serve.

Cook's Tip

Dried fruits, especially apricots are good in curries. This is an excellent one to serve as an accompaniment to a lamb curry as part of an Indian-style meal. It is also good cold, served with hot pitta bread.

Cook's Tip

Different versions of yogurt curry are made all over India. Delicious as it is, diced root vegetables or cauliflower florets can be added – cooking times may have to be adjusted. It is ideal with a dry vegetable or meat curry.

Desserts

Desserts as westerners know them are uncommon in the Far East. Most Orientals will finish their meal with a serving of fresh tropical fruit. If a dessert is served in Japan or China it will usually be as part of a banquet and may be served between courses; the Indians are more noted for their sweet meal offerings and sweetmeats which can be eaten at the end of a meal, taken when visiting on festival days or nibbled like a snack.

249 | Semolina Barfi

(Illustrated on front jacket)

Preparation time
10 minutes, plus cooling time

Cooking time
about 20 minutes

Serves 4–6

Calories
470–310 per portion

You will need
50 g/2 oz fine semolina
100 g/4 oz sugar
450 ml/¾ pint milk
50 g/2 oz butter
10 cardamoms, crushed
75 g/3 oz blanched almonds, halved and toasted

Place the semolina and sugar in a heavy-based pan and stir in the milk gradually until smooth. Add the butter in small pieces. Bring to the boil, stirring, then simmer for 3–4 minutes, until thickened, stirring occasionally to prevent sticking. Add the crushed cardamoms and continue cooking for another 10 minutes or until the mixture leaves the sides of the pan.

Spread on a buttered plate or dish to a thickness of 1 to 1.5 cm/½ to 1 inch. Leave until almost cold and then decorate with the almonds. Serve cold, cut into slices or squares.

250 | Baked Bananas

Preparation time
10 minutes, plus 30 minutes marinating time

Cooking time
15–20 minutes

Oven temperature
180 C, 350 F, gas 4

Serves 4

Calories
250 per portion

You will need
50 g/2 oz seedless raisins
50 ml/2 fl oz rum
4 bananas, peeled
25 g/1 oz butter
50 g/2 oz demerara sugar
50 ml/2 fl oz orange juice
2 teaspoons grated lemon rind

Place the raisins in a small bowl, add the rum and then marinate for 30 minutes.

Place each banana on a 20-cm/8-inch square of foil, then dot each with a quarter of the butter. Sprinkle evenly with the raisins, rum, sugar, orange juice and lemon rind and seal the packages securely. Bake for 15–20 minutes. Serve at once.

Cook's Tip

Cardamoms are aromatic seed pods that come in 3 varieties: white, green and large black. The green is probably the most perfumed. The whole pod is used to flavour rice and meat dishes and then discarded, or the pod is opened and the seed removed and crushed for sprinkling on sweets and vegetables.

Cook's Tip

Lemon juice can be used instead of rum in the above recipe. Serve with a scoop of ice cream if liked.

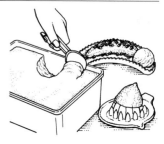

251 | *Fried Bread in Saffron and Pistachio Sauce*

Preparation time
15 minutes, plus 1 hour chilling time

Cooking time
about 5 minutes

Serves 6

Calories
630 per portion

You will need
1 small loaf white bread, crusts removed
vegetable oil for deep frying
1 teaspoon saffron threads
600 ml/1 pint milk, warmed
225 g/8 oz clear honey
50 g/2 oz shelled pistachios, coarsely chopped
25 g/1 oz blanched almonds, chopped
300 ml/½ pint single cream
5–6 drops rose water

Cut the bread into 2.5-cm/1-inch thick slices, then cut each slice lengthways. Heat the oil in a deep fat frier and deep fry the bread until golden. Drain on absorbent kitchen paper and keep hot.

Put the saffron in a cup and cover with some of the milk. Add the honey to the remaining milk and heat until melted, then add the nuts. Strain in the saffron-coloured milk, stir and remove from the heat. Cool slightly.

Stir in the cream and rose water. Put the bread in the serving bowl, pour over the sauce and chill in the refrigerator for at least 1 hour before serving.

252 | *Fruit Fritters*

Preparation time
10 minutes

Cooking time
about 15 minutes

Serves 8

Calories
300 per portion

You will need
2 large, firm eating apples
2 bananas
1 egg
4 tablespoons cornflour
vegetable oil for deep frying
100 g/4 oz sugar
3 tablespoons sesame oil
1 tablespoon sesame seeds

For the decoration
lime slices
banana slices

Peel and core the apples, then cut each into 8 pieces. Halve the bananas lengthways, then cut each half into 3–4 pieces. Beat the egg, then blend in the cornflour and enough cold water to make a smooth batter.

Heat the oil, dip each fruit in the batter then deep fry in the oil in a deep fat frier for 2–3 minutes. Drain on absorbent kitchen paper. Heat the sugar and sesame oil in a pan over a low heat for 5 minutes. Add 3 tablespoons water and stir for 2 minutes. Add the fruit fritters and the sesame seeds and stir slowly, until each fritter is covered with syrup. As soon as the syrup has caramelized, remove the fritters and plunge into a bowl of cold water to harden the 'toffee'.

Serve decorated with lime and banana slices.

Cook's Tip

This is very much a king of Mogul recipes. Although rich, it is refreshing to eat at the end of a large feast, when served chilled.

Cook's Tip

Undoubtedly, fruit fritters are one of the most famous Chinese dessert dishes served in Peking-style restaurants. Apple and banana seem to be the most popular fruits, but any other firm-fleshed fruit or canned fruit could be used.

253 | *Banana Fritters*

Preparation time
10 minutes

Cooking time
about 5 minutes

Serves 8

Calories
250 per portion

You will need
100 g/4 oz self-raising flour
40 g/1½ oz rice flour
½ teaspoon salt
finely grated rind of 1 lime
   (optional)
vegetable oil for deep frying
8 small bananas
lime wedges for serving
caster sugar for serving

Sift the flours and salt into a bowl. Add about 200 ml/ 7 fl oz water to make a smooth coating batter, then stir in the grated lime rind, if using.

Heat the oil in a wok or deep fat frier. Meanwhile, peel the bananas, spear them one at a time with a skewer and dip into the batter until evenly coated. Deep fry, in batches, in the hot oil until crisp and golden. Drain on absorbent kitchen paper.

Serve hot with lime wedges and sprinkled over with caster sugar.

254 | *Rice Fritters*

Preparation time
10 minutes

Cooking time
about 5–10 minutes

Makes about 20

Calories
100 per fritter

You will need
160 g/5½ oz cooked medium-
   grain rice
2 eggs, beaten
3 tablespoons sugar
½ teaspoon vanilla essence
50 g/2 oz plain flour
1 tablespoon baking powder
pinch of salt
25 g/1 oz desiccated coconut
vegetable oil for deep frying
sifted icing sugar for sprinkling

Put the rice, eggs, sugar and vanilla in a bowl and mix well. Sift together the flour, baking powder and salt, then stir into the rice mixture. Stir in the coconut.

Heat the oil in a deep-fat frier to 180 C/350 F (just before it starts to sizzle). Drop tablespoonfuls of the mixture into the hot oil, one at a time, and deep fry until golden on all sides. Drain on absorbent kitchen paper.

Transfer to a warmed serving dish and sprinkle with a generous amount of icing sugar. Serve hot.

Cook's Tip

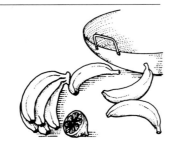

If possible, buy very small bananas – sometimes called 'apple bananas' – for these fritters: they look better than the larger ones and are usually sweeter in flavour.

Cook's Tip

In many Asian countries rice is often used as an ingredient for desserts. These are not always eaten after a meal, in the western manner, but may be served as a snack between meals.

255 | *Doughnut Spirals in Syrup*

Preparation time
15 minutes, plus
overnight standing

Cooking time
about 10 minutes

Makes 20–24

Calories
270 per spiral

You will need
275 g/10 oz plain flour
40 g/1½ oz rice flour
pinch of baking powder
½ teaspoon salt
175 ml/6 fl oz water
vegetable oil for deep frying

For the syrup
1 litre/1¾ pints water
200 g/8 oz sugar
pinch of cream of tartar
½ teaspoon rose water
½ teaspoon yellow or red food
	colouring (optional)

Sift the flours, baking powder and salt into a bowl. Gradually add the water and beat to a smooth batter. Cover and chill overnight.

To make the syrup, put the water, sugar and cream of tartar in a heavy-based pan and heat to dissolve the sugar. Add the rose water and food colouring if used.

Heat the oil, put the batter in a piping bag fitted with a large plain nozzle and pipe spirals, about 10 cm/4 inches in diameter, into the hot oil. Deep fry for about 3 minutes until crisp, then drain on absorbent kitchen paper.

Immerse the spirals in the syrup for 30 seconds while still warm. Serve warm or cold.

Cook's Tip

These pretzel-like sweets or dessert are a joy if eaten sweet and warm. In Indian cities, they are sold at open stalls where, by the light of a hissing Tilley lamp, the spirals are deep-fried especially for you.

256 | *Deep-Fried Sweet Potato Balls*

Preparation time
10 minutes

Cooking time
about 25 minutes

Serves 4–6

Calories
450–350 per portion

You will need
450 g/1 lb sweet potatoes
100 g/4 oz glutinous or sweet rice
	flour
50 g/2 oz brown sugar
50 g/2 oz sesame seeds
oil for deep frying

Put the potatoes in a pan, cover with water and bring to the boil. Reduce the heat and simmer for 15–20 minutes or until tender. Drain and peel. Mash the potatoes, then beat in the rice flour and sugar.

With dampened hands, form the mixture into walnut-sized balls. Roll each ball in sesame seeds.

Heat the oil to 160 C/325 F and deep fry the potato balls until golden. Drain on absorbent kitchen paper, then serve hot.

Cook's Tip

This recipe can also be made from yams instead of the sweet potatoes. A yam is a large sweet tuberous root with a moist texture. It resembles a sweet potato and is cooked in the same way.

257 | Cream Cheese Balls in Syrup

Preparation time
15 minutes, plus making panir

Cooking time
2¼ hours

Makes 12–15

Calories
400 per ball

You will need
1 recipe Panir (see Cook's Tip)
75 g/3 oz blanched almonds, chopped
115 g/4½ oz semolina
12–15 cubes sugar

For the syrup
1 litre/1¾ pints water
200 g/8 oz sugar
pinch of cream of tartar
½ teaspoon rose water

Stir the panir to a smooth paste, then add the almonds and semolina. Knead well until smooth.

When the palm of the hand is greasy, mould the paste. Break the dough into 12–15 pieces, about the size of walnuts. Shape into balls, moulding each one around a sugar cube.

To make the syrup, put all the ingredients except the rose water in a heavy-based pan and heat gently until the sugar dissolves. Bring to the boil, add the balls of dough, then lower the heat and simmer very gently for 2 hours. Stir in the rose water, then serve hot or cold.

Cook's Tip

To make panir, a simple curd cheese, put 2.4 litres/4 pints milk in a pan and bring to the boil. Remove from the heat, leave to cool to 37C/98F. Beat in 500 ml/17 fl oz natural yogurt, 4 teaspoons lemon juice and 1 tablespoon salt.

Leave in a warm place for 12 hours. Strain through muslin for 30 minutes, then squeeze out as much liquid as possible. Shape in the cloth and place under a heavy weight for 3 hours; cut into cubes to use.

258 | Almond Junket

Preparation time
15 minutes, plus 2–3 hours chilling time

Cooking time
about 5–10 minutes

Serves 4

Calories
280 per portion

You will need
15 g/½ oz agar-agar or isinglass (see Cook's Tip)
4 tablespoons sugar
300 ml/½ pint milk
1 teaspoon almond flavouring
1 (400-g/14-oz) can apricots or mixed fruit salad
50 g/2 oz white grapes, peeled and seeded

Dissolve the agar-agar or isinglass in 300 ml/½ pint water over a gentle heat. Dissolve the sugar in 300 ml/½ pint water in a separate saucepan, then combine with the dissolved setting agent and add the milk and almond flavouring. Pour into a large serving bowl and leave until cold. Chill for at least 2–3 hours until set.

To serve, cut the junket into small cubes and place in a serving bowl. Pour the canned fruit and syrup over the junket, add the grapes and mix well. Serve chilled.

Cook's Tip

Agar-agar or isinglass is used as a setting agent. It is possible to use gelatine instead. Use 25 g/1 oz powdered gelatine and dissolve in the water according to the packet instructions.

259 | *Vermicelli Pudding*

Preparation time
5 minutes

Cooking time
20–25 minutes

Serves 6

Calories
440 per portion

You will need
100 g/4 oz ghee
100 g/4 oz vermicelli
750 ml/1¼ pints milk
15 cardamoms
225 g/8 oz clear honey
100 g/4 oz sultanas

Heat the ghee in a heavy-based pan and add the vermicelli, breaking it into 4-cm/1½-inch pieces. Fry gently for 5–6 minutes, then pour on the milk and bring to the boil.

Remove the seeds from the cardamoms and crush in a pestle and mortar. Sprinkle into the pan and add the honey, spoon by spoon. Stir well until the honey has melted. Cook for a further 10–15 minutes, then stir in the sultanas. Serve hot or chilled.

260 | *Indian Fruit Salad*

Preparation time
5 minutes, plus 3 hours soaking time

Cooking time
20 minutes

Serves 4

Calories
100 per portion

You will need
225 g/8 oz dried tamarind
1 teaspoon chilli powder
sugar
2 green chillies, thinly sliced (optional)
2.5 cm/1 inch piece root ginger, peeled and cut into fine strips
1 each pear, apple and banana or guava, mango and any other fruit, cut into small pieces

Put the tamarind in a bowl, cover with boiling water and set aside for 3 hours or overnight.

Tip the tamarind and water into a sieve placed over a saucepan and, using your fingers, push through as much pulp as possible. Discard the husk and seeds.

Add the chilli powder, sugar to taste and simmer gently for 15–20 minutes. Pour into a bowl and set aside to cool.

Stir in the chillies. (For a savoury accompaniment use ginger and fruit.) Cover and chill before serving.

Cook's Tip

When Muslims visit each other on feast days, they are always asked to partake of some food. Invariably a large bowl of vermicelli pudding is made, which is dipped into throughout the day as visitors come and go.

Cook's Tip

This is a spicy fruit salad, also known as Fruit Chat, that can be served as a sharp dessert but is also served as an accompaniment to a main meal. It can be made with dried fruit that has been soaked overnight.

261 | *Eight-Jewel Rice Pudding*

Preparation time
20 minutes

Cooking time
1¼–1½ hours

Serves 6

Calories
550 per portion

You will need
350 g/12 oz pudding rice
4 tablespoons caster sugar
50 g/2 oz unsalted butter
100 g/4 oz glacé cherries, chopped
50 g/2 oz crystallized orange peel, chopped
25 g/1 oz each angelica, walnuts and blanched almonds, chopped
50 g/2 oz seedless raisins, chopped
5 tablespoons sweet red bean paste

For the syrup
(see Cook's Tip)

Rinse the rice, drain and put in a pan with enough water to cover. Simmer for 15 minutes; drain. Stir in the sugar and half the butter.

Use the remaining butter to grease a 900-ml/1½-pint pudding basin, then line with a thin layer of rice. Press a little of each fruit and nut into this to make a decorative pattern. Mix the remaining rice, fruit and nuts. Spoon alternate layers of this rice mixture and bean paste into the basin finishing with a layer of rice. Press down firmly. Cover with greaseproof paper and pleated foil and steam for 1–1¼ hours.

Turn the pudding out on to a serving dish and serve hot with the warm syrup.

Cook's Tip

To make the syrup for this recipe, bring 300 ml/½ pint water mixed with 50 g/2 oz sugar to the boil, stirring constantly. Remove from the heat and add a few drops of almond essence, vanilla essence, rose water or orange *water. Pour over the pudding and serve hot.*

262 | *Almond Fruit Salad*

Preparation time
15 minutes, plus chilling time

Cooking time
10 minutes

Serves 4–6

Calories
250–170 per portion

You will need
4 dessert apples, cored
4 peaches, skinned and stoned
100 g/4 oz strawberries
4 slices pineapple
100 g/4 oz lychees, skinned

For the almond syrup
1 tablespoon cornflour
2 tablespoons water
2 tablespoons ground almonds
450 ml/¾ pint water
3 tablespoons sugar

First make the syrup. Blend the cornflour with 2 tablespoons water. Put the almonds, remaining water, blended cornflour and sugar into a pan and mix well. Gradually bring to the boil, stirring, then simmer for 10 minutes, stirring constantly. Remove from the heat and leave to cool, stirring occasionally so as to prevent a skin forming.

Slice the apples, peaches and strawberries; cut the pineapple into cubes. Put all the fruit in a bowl and mix well. Spoon over the almond syrup; chill before serving.

Cook's Tip

Toss the apples in a little lemon juice after slicing to prevent them turning brown.

263 | *Caramel Apples*

Preparation time
15 minutes

Cooking time
5–7 minutes

Serves 4

Calories
520 per portion

You will need
2 egg whites
6 tablespoons self-raising flour
plain flour for coating
4 large dessert apples, peeled,
    cored and each cut into 8
    pieces
oil for deep frying

For the caramel coating
175 g/6 oz sugar
3 tablespoons water
25 g/1 oz unsalted butter
1–2 tablespoons sesame seeds,
    lightly toasted

Lightly beat the egg whites, then beat in the flour to form a smooth batter. Sprinkle a little plain flour over the apple slices, then coat with the batter.

Heat the oil in a wok or deep frier and deep fry the apples for about 5–7 minutes, until golden. Drain on absorbent kitchen paper.

To make the caramel coating, put the sugar and water in a heavy pan and stir over a gentle heat until dissolved. Add the butter, increase the heat and continue cooking until the mixture has caramelized to a golden colour. Add the sesame seeds and apples and stir quickly to coat.

Dip the apples into cold water to harden the caramel, drain, then serve at once.

264 | *Fruit Custard*

Preparation time
10 minutes

Cooking time
about 15 minutes

Serves 4

Calories
320 per portion

You will need
3 eggs
4 tablespoons caster sugar
300 ml/½ pint water
350 g/12 oz pineapple, finely
    shredded
50 g/2 oz dates, finely shredded
75 g/3 oz crystallized fruit, finely
    shredded
25 g/1 oz dried figs, finely
    shredded
1 tablespoon arrowroot powder

Beat the eggs, 1 tablespoon sugar and 4 tablespoons of the water together in a deep ovenproof dish. Place in a steamer and steam for 7–8 minutes until the mixture is set.

Mix all the fruit together and spoon over the egg custard. Mix the arrowroot and remaining sugar together, then gradually blend in the remaining water. Bring to the boil, stirring, and cook for 2 minutes. Spoon over the fruit and serve hot or cold.

Cook's Tip

Sesame seeds are tiny, creamy, yellow flat seeds with a nutty flavour. They are used to make sesame oil but make a flavoursome addition to many sweet and savoury dishes in the seed form.

Cook's Tip

Arrowroot is a fine powdered starch which when used as a thickening produces a clear cooked mixture. It is possible in the recipe above to use cornflour instead, but the result will be a little more cloudy.

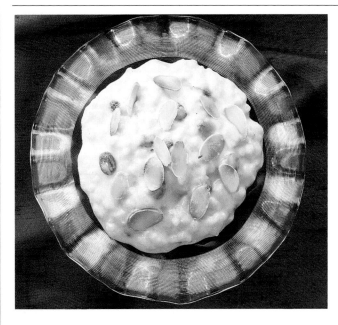

265 | *Kheer*

Preparation time
5 minutes, plus cooling time

Cooking time
1–1¼ hours

Serves 4

Calories
490 per portion

You will need
75 g/3 oz long-grain rice
1.8 litres/3 pints milk
50 g/2 oz sultanas
caster sugar
150 ml/¼ pint single cream
flaked almonds to decorate

Put the rice and 1 litre/1¾ pints of the milk in a heavy-based pan. Cook gently at simmering point for 45–60 minutes, until most of the milk has been absorbed.

Add the remaining milk and sultanas, stir well and continue simmering until thickened. Remove from the heat and stir in sugar to taste.

Leave until completely cold, stirring occasionally to prevent a skin from forming, then stir in the cream.

Turn the mixture into small dishes and serve cold, sprinkled with flaked almonds.

Cook's Tip

The Kheer could be sprinkled with lightly crushed cardamom seeds instead of the almonds if liked.

266 | *Coconut Ice Cream*

Preparation time
15 minutes, plus 2–3 hours freezing time

Cooking time
15–20 minutes

Makes about 900 ml/1½ pints

Total calories
2200

You will need
350 ml/12 fl oz milk
75 g/3 oz desiccated coconut
350 ml/12 fl oz single cream
2 eggs
2 egg yolks
100 g/4 oz sugar
¼ teaspoon salt

Scald the milk, coconut and cream in a heavy-based pan over a low heat – about 15–20 minutes. Push through a fine sieve, pressing out as much of the coconut juice as possible. Discard the coconut.

Beat the eggs and egg yolks with an electric beater until thick and mousse-like. Place over a pan of simmering water, stir in some of the coconut cream mixture, then the remainder and cook until the mixture will coat the back of a spoon. Cool quickly, then pour into freezer trays and freeze until mushy. Beat again to break up the ice crystals, return to the freezer trays and freeze until firm, about 2–3 hours.

Scoop into chilled glasses to serve.

Cook's Tip

Take the ice cream from the refrigerator about 30 minutes before serving – this helps to soften the ice cream so that it is easy to scoop.

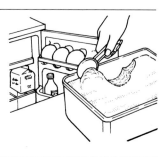

267 | Carrot Halwa

Preparation time
10 minutes

Cooking time
25–30 minutes

Serves 4–6

Calories
520–350 per portion

You will need
1.2 litres/2 pints milk
225 g/8 oz carrots, finely grated
75 g/3 oz butter
1 tablespoon golden syrup
100 g/4 oz sugar
50 g/2 oz sultanas or raisins
1 teaspoon cardamom seeds,
    crushed

Place the milk and carrots in a heavy-based pan and cook over a high heat, stirring occasionally, until the liquid has evaporated.

Add the butter, syrup, sugar and fruit. Stir until the butter and sugar have melted, then cook for 15–20 minutes, stirring frequently, until the mixture starts to leave the sides of the pan.

Pour into a shallow buttered dish and spread evenly. Sprinkle with the crushed cardamoms. Cut into slices and serve warm or cold.

268 | Walnut Sweet

Preparation time
about 15 minutes,
including soaking time

Cooking time
5–10 minutes

Serves 4–6

Calories
500–350 per portion

You will need
100 g/4 oz shelled walnuts
3 tablespoons oil
75 g/3 oz dates, stoned
900 ml/1½ pints water
150 g/5 oz sugar
40 g/1½ oz ground rice
3 tablespoons milk
apple flower to decorate (see
    Cook's Tip)

Soak the walnuts in boiling water for 10 minutes, drain and remove the skins; dry on absorbent kitchen paper.

Heat the oil in a wok or deep frying pan, add the walnuts and fry quickly until lightly browned (take care not to burn them). Drain on absorbent kitchen paper.

Grind the nuts and dates in a blender, food processor or fine mincer. Bring the water to the boil and stir in the nut mixture and sugar. Blend the ground rice with the milk and add to the nut mixture. Bring back to the boil, stirring, and cook for 2 minutes until thickened.

Spoon into a warmed serving dish, decorate with an apple flower and serve hot.

Cook's Tip

It is said there are as many halwas in India as there are cities, and each centre of population guards the reputation of its sweetmeat. Often halwa is used as a sort of culinary envoy, being sent all over the world. It is well worth making at home, although it is said that the art of the halwai (halwa maker) is inherited and cannot ever be learned!

Cook's Tip

To make an apple flower, thinly pare the rind from a small apple, taking care to keep it in one piece. Tightly curl the skin into a circle to make a flower shape and position on the dish.

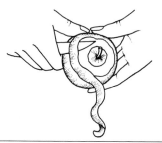

269 | *Bean and Kiwi Fool*

Preparation time
10 minutes, plus overnight soaking time and chilling time

Cooking time
45–60 minutes

Serves 8

Calories
260 per portion

You will need
175 g/6 oz moong beans, soaked in cold water overnight
100 ml/4 fl oz milk
300 ml/½ pint double cream
1½ tablespoons brown sugar
2 tablespoons sake (rice wine)
1 teaspoon vanilla flavouring
2 kiwi fruit, peeled and puréed, to decorate

Drain the beans and rinse, then place in a large pan and cover with fresh cold water. Bring to the boil, half cover and cook for 45–60 minutes until tender. Drain well.

Put the cooked beans in a liquidizer or food processor and work to a purée. Add the milk and 100 ml/4 fl oz of the cream and mix to a thick batter, then add the sugar, rice wine and vanilla. Pour into 8 individual glasses or bowls and chill for at least 2 hours.

To serve, pour a little of the kiwi fruit purée on top of each pudding. Whip the remaining cream until thick, then spoon or pipe on top. Serve well chilled.

270 | *Caramel Custards with Lime*

Preparation time
20 minutes, plus chilling time

Cooking time
about 1 hour

Oven temperature
160 C, 325 F, gas 3

Makes 8

Calories
280 per portion

You will need
225 g/8 oz granulated sugar

For the custard
1 (410-g/14½-oz) can evaporated milk
300 ml/½ pint milk
5 eggs
1 tablespoon caster sugar
finely grated rind of 2 limes

Put the sugar in a pan, add 8 tablespoons water and heat to dissolve. Boil, without stirring until the mixture turns a rich golden caramel colour. Immediately pour a little into 8 warmed 150-ml/¼-pint ramekins and swirl to coat the base and sides.

Warm the evaporated milk and milk together in a pan, without boiling. Whisk the eggs with the sugar, then slowly whisk in the warmed milk. Strain, then stir in the lime rind and pour into the ramekin dishes.

Stand in a roasting tin with cold water to come halfway up the sides of the dishes and bake for about 45 minutes or until set. Remove from the water and leave to cool, then chill for at least 2 hours.

Turn out to serve on individual serving dishes, or serve in the ramekins.

Cook's Tip

It is possible to buy moong beans with the husks removed, but the texture given by the moong bean skins is good in this Vietnamese pudding.

Cook's Tip

This variation of crème caramel shows a glimpse of the Spanish influence on Philippino cuisine. It has a delicious bitter-sweet flavour that makes an ideal dessert to serve after a robust or rich main course dish.

271 | Indian Ice Cream with Pistachios

Preparation time
10 minutes, plus 3–4 hours freezing time

Cooking time
45 minutes

Serves 6–8

Calories
370–280 per portion

You will need
300 ml / ½ pint double cream
300 ml / ½ pint milk
1 (400-g/14-oz) can condensed milk
1 tablespoon clear honey
2 tablespoons chopped pistachios
2 teaspoons rose water
green food colouring (optional)

Heat the cream, milk, condensed milk and honey together in a heavy-based pan. Bring gently to the boil, stirring constantly, then simmer for 45 minutes over a very low heat. Remove from the heat, sprinkle in the pistachios and rose water, then add a little food colouring if liked. Allow to cool.

Pour the mixture into a shallow 900-ml/1½-pint freezer container or 6–8 kulfi moulds and freeze for 3–4 hours. Remove from the freezer and leave to stand at room temperature for 20–30 minutes to soften.

To serve, turn out of the kulfi moulds (see Cook's Tip) or cut into squares.

272 | Chinese Fruit Salad

Preparation time
20–25 minutes, plus 2 hours chilling time

Serves 4

Calories
100–200 per portion

You will need
1 large honeydew melon
4–5 types fresh or canned fruit, with the syrup from the can (see Cook's Tip)

Cut the honeydew melon in half and scoop out and discard the seeds. Cut the flesh into small chunks and reserve the shell.

Prepare the other fruit, leaving it whole if small, otherwise separating it into segments or cutting it into small chunks as with the melon.

Mix the pieces of melon with the fruit and canned syrup. Pack the melon shell with this mixture, then cover tightly with cling film. Chill for at least 2 hours in the refrigerator before serving.

Cook's Tip

This recipe calls for the inclusion of condensed milk, and to make it even richer, double cream. Traditionally, this Indian ice cream would be served in kulfi moulds, which are small and conical in shape and available from most specialist cook shops. To turn out the ice cream, briefly dip the kulfi mould, upside down, in warm water, then invert on to a serving dish.

Cook's Tip

Choose from kiwi fruit, lychees, strawberries, pineapple, pears, apples, peaches, grapes, cherries and tangerines. For the best effect you should have at least 4 different types of fruit.